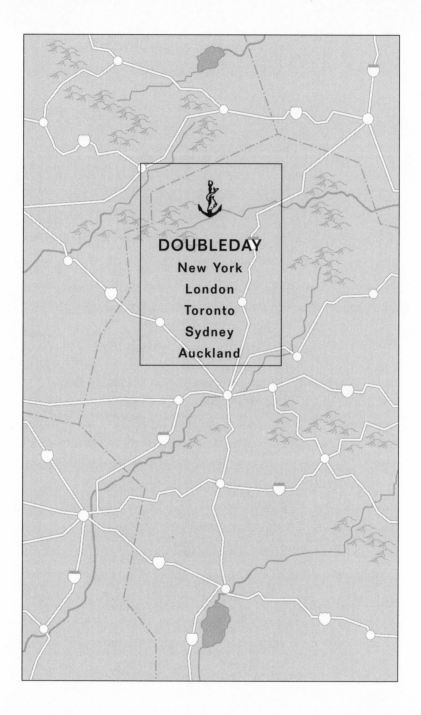

DOUBLEDAY

New York
London
Toronto
Sydney
Auckland

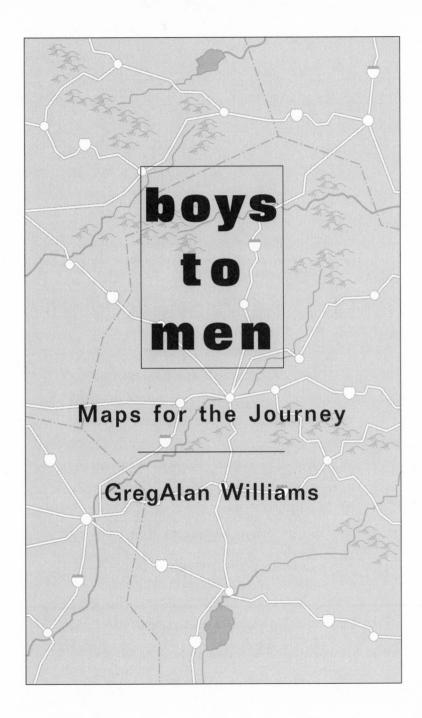

boys
to
men

Maps for the Journey

GregAlan Williams

PUBLISHED BY DOUBLEDAY
a division of Bantam Doubleday Dell Publishing Group, Inc.
1540 Broadway, New York, New York 10036

DOUBLEDAY and the portrayal of an anchor with a dolphin are trademarks
of Doubleday, a division of Bantam Doubleday Dell Publishing Group, Inc.

Book design by Maria Carella

Library of Congress Cataloging-in-Publication Data

Williams, GregAlan.
Boys to men : maps for the journey / GregAlan Williams.–
1st ed.
p.   cm.
1. Boys.   2. Parenting.   3. Masculinity (Psychology)
4. Fatherless family.   5. Fathers and sons.   I. Title.
HQ775.A58   1997
649'.132–DC20   96-32492   CIP

ISBN 0-385-48687-1

February 1997

3   5   7   9   10   8   6   4

This book is dedicated with great love and gratitude
to my mother
and with great hopefulness and expectation
to my sons
and
your sons

contents

section 2

section 3

preface

Experience may be the best teacher,
but thank God it's not the only teacher.

—DETROIT NICK

Three or four years ago I went hiking with my eldest son, Travis, in a canyon that has been the backdrop for hundreds of movies and TV shows. From almost any angle it looks as if the canyon's rustic hills and roads, and the huge cave at its center, are smack dab from the middle of the Old West, a Korean War battlefield, or maybe even somewhere on the moon. But actually the canyon is right in the heart of Hollywood.

Travis had run on ahead. His destination: a rocky hill thirty or forty yards away. As I watched him dart up the path a sudden hot rush of anger blew over me. It lasted only a moment. After it passed, I was left with an overwhelming sadness that nearly brought me to tears. Inside that sadness I was able to see what had been inside my anger only a moment before—a deep and abiding jealousy of my son. The boy in front of me was blessed with a good father to take him hiking. A compassionate man with whom his connection was sure and unbreakable. A man in whose face the boy could see his own and perhaps even catch a glimpse of what, and who, he could become. This boy, my son, was experiencing a kind of love I had not. And for one brief moment I had hated him for it.

Smiling through my sadness I hurried to catch up with Travis. I caught him just as he was beginning to climb the rocky hill. Together we made our way up the slope shoulder to shoulder. I watched him grin as he went, and he watched me too. As we reached the top I saw in my mind's eye myself looking back at myself. At that moment two sons stood on top of the hill. And I was father to us both.

For many years now I have taken an active role in my own "fathering." This book is part of that ongoing responsibility—a conscious effort to exercise the awareness I received on that hill. If my father had spoken to me when I was a boy, what might he have said? What would he have told me about being a man? Perhaps he would have had little to say. Even so, he might have been able to help Mother make my journey a little clearer.

I imagine I tend to romanticize the relationship between father and son a bit. But then, I suspect a hungry man's dream of eggs and bacon is a vision of pure love.

It is in love that I write. To my sons, to you, to your sons, and to myself. So that we all may father each other.

boys to men

introduction

---

*Every generation needs the instruction
and insights of past generations
in order to forge its own vision.*

—JESSE JACKSON

Each one of us has to travel his own journey. Still, it is important to share with each other the things we learn on our journeys. While listening to the dangerous twists and wrong turns in
someone else's travels may not keep us from walking directly
into some of the same dangers or making some of the same
mistakes, hearing other men's and women's stories may provide
us with maps for our own journey. If we should find ourselves in
a bad land or on a rocky road, we can open the map of someone
else's experience and, at the very least, know where we are.
Looking at maps from another man's journey can tell us when

we are about to cross an invisible border into hostile territory. Even if we choose to continue into the bad land, or along that rocky road, the experiences of others provide us with a clear picture of the size and shape of the dangers that lie ahead. Knowing about these dangers may scare us into turning around and heading in the other direction, or they just may make us wiser about the path we're on. If we are lost we can use these maps to identify the ground we're standing on. Then we can use our maps to get us back on our journey's right path.

I have a friend named Barry who is a professional body builder. Now Barry's a lot younger than I am but he's already lifted a lot more weight than I ever will. Every now and then Barry and I work out together. He doesn't talk much when he's working out, but when he does talk, I listen. Most of the time after listening to Barry I come away with a map of information that can guide me on my journey in the weight room. Not long ago Barry and I were doing some chest work. My normal routine was to jump right into semi-heavy bench presses. Barry, however, suggested we start out with very light repetitions on the pec deck to warm up our muscles before going to the bench. While we were warming up Barry told me about the time he injured a muscle in his chest benching a heavy weight. His injury, he said, was caused by not warming up properly. The injury had been painful and slow to heal. According to Barry, it was several weeks before he was able to compete again. I listened to Barry closely and added that information to my map. At the start of my next chest workout I stood still for a moment and reflected on what Barry had said about pulling that chest muscle. In some ways I pulled Barry's map out of a place in my mind that's like a bag where I keep things I need for my journey. I opened up that map and studied it before starting on that day's workout. I saw that Barry had pulled a muscle once by not warming up properly and I worried the same thing might happen to me. So I took a few moments, went over to the pec deck, and did some light warm-ups. And you know what? So far I haven't pulled a muscle. At least, not in my chest.

One question that comes up when listening to other people's experiences is: "How do we know a guy is telling the truth about his journey?" Someone could tell you a particular spot on his journey was warm, sunny, and enjoyable when actually that spot was like a scene from a horror movie. People are people, and sometimes all of us like to make certain parts of our journeys seem a lot more successful or exciting than they really were. When I was a boy I used to ask military veterans to tell me about the war they were in. Most of the time they'd tell me about how hard basic training was and about a couple of the girls they met overseas. These guys would talk about the big battles I had already read about in the history books and they'd marvel at the ships, tanks, planes, and artillery they'd seen. But not once did one of those veterans talk to me about how they felt watching their friends get killed. They never talked about being seventeen or eighteen and scared to death in a damp hole in the ground listening to mortars leave their tubes. They never described the feeling that there was nothing they could do but sit, wait, and hope it didn't hit where they were sitting and blow them apart. Of course I understand now why those veterans were so reluctant to talk about these things. After all, I was a kid and they didn't want to scare me. I was also a boy and that meant that one day somebody might call on me to sit in that damp hole and wait for those incoming mortars. Maybe they didn't want to discourage me from doing my *"duty."* However, it would have been nice if they had told me what to expect so that I could make an informed choice about whether or not to offer my limbs or my life for my country or a cause. And then too, those vets couldn't really talk about being scared because men are supposed to be brave and fearless.

I found out much later that war isn't just about basic training and girls. I didn't get to this truth solely from the maps of the vets. Instead I compared that information with other people's experiences. I cross-referenced their maps with other maps. In order to find out whether someone is telling the truth about a journey you need to compare the information on his or her map with the maps of other folks. Try to gather as many maps as you can. I am a pilot and when I fly I use several different sources to determine the route of my flight. I start out with a standard flight chart—a map—and I draw a line from the airport where I am taking off to the airport where I intend to land. I look at all the different landmarks along my route. I pay close attention to the elevation of the terrain. Then, I may get another chart that shows the same route on a larger scale. On that chart everything looks bigger and farther apart and I can see the landmarks and the terrain much more clearly. After studying those charts I get a weather chart. This map shows me what the weather patterns are like over my route. Studying the weather chart can give me a good idea of where I might run into thunderstorms, rain, and other weather conditions that could cause trouble during my flight. In addition to all this, I call the Flight Service Station to get a weather briefing and information about closed runways and inoperative navigation equipment along my route. This is important if I get lost or need to make an emergency landing. Finally, I take all this information and put it together to determine the truth about my flight. The first two charts I looked at may have told me the route looked clear. One of the weather charts may have told me a storm in the area was moving away from my route of flight. The weather service might say that strong winds generated by that storm were also in the area. Flight Service also recommends I find a different route. To be on the safe side, I talk to other pilots who have just flown the route recently and they tell me the air was bumpy and there was some rain during the flight. So now, based on *all* this information, I might determine that the flight is dangerous. There is a possibility I could run into a storm that might cause a problem. When I put the information from all these maps together—the flight charts, the weather maps, the Flight Service's warning, and the other pilots' experiences—I can make a pretty good decision about what route to fly, when to fly it, or whether I shouldn't just drive to where I'm going.

The more we listen to the experiences of others and the

more maps we gather, the more information we will have to make the journey from boyhood into manhood. As we compare the information we receive from these maps we can begin to make a fair determination about which maps offer the most reliable information. Just as in planning a flight, the most reliable information for our journey will not come from one source but from many sources. Comparing maps will help us to know how, when, and in what direction we should travel. Cross-referencing can also tell us whether a man is telling the truth about his journey. And truth, gentlemen, is essential food for our journey.

The experiences of another man's journey can do more than guide us away from danger. These maps can also guide us to the good stuff. As I travel, I listen regularly to the experiences of others. The maps I find in their experience show me how to get to the good stuff and how to avoid the bad stuff. Sometimes I can put another man's experience to use the moment I receive it. If not, I rarely throw it away. You never know when that map will come in handy. I simply put the map in my mental bag so I can find it when I need it. Gentlemen, throughout our lives we should keep putting our own experiences and the experiences of others in a bag that we carry with us on our journey. The maps of these journeys will form an atlas that we can refer to as we travel. Let's say you're traveling in Africa, and using a world atlas to find your way around the continent's many countries and cities. You don't tear out the maps of the countries and cities of Asia, Europe, and the Americas just because you're not traveling in those places at that moment. Of course not. You use the maps of Africa that you need right now and the other maps of the world you keep in the book. When your trip to Africa is over you put the entire atlas in the bag where you can find it, because you never know exactly where your next trip will take you. When it's time to travel again that atlas will tell you exactly how to get where you're going and what the terrain will be like when you arrive, no matter where you decide to go.

Occasionally on your journey you'll find yourself going down the same road again. It might be a good road. It might be a bad road. Since you've been down the road before you can use your own map to tell you what lies ahead. All you have to do is look at your map! This seems simple, but it's not. For some reason I am forgetful when it comes to remembering roads on my journey that I've traveled before. It's like this: the first time I hit a particular road I get into some real rough going. Fortunately, however, that first time I get turned around and eventually I get back on a smoother track. Then, a few months or maybe a few years later, not really realizing it, I start right back down that same old road all over again. Don't get me wrong, when I turn onto the road, I definitely notice a few things that seem familiar. And something says to me, "Hey, dude, haven't you seen this terrain before? Doesn't this road get hard and steep after a while?" My head asks myself this question. Good sense tells me something about this road is familiar—to look at the map! But I don't. That's because the first part of the road is smooth and easy. The scenery is nice to look at. The first part of the road is exciting and fun. But if I had taken the time to look at my map I would easily recognize the hard going that was waiting for me ahead.

Years ago, whenever I got a speeding ticket I never paid it by the due date. Then, because I failed to pay the ticket, a warrant would be issued for my arrest. So if I was cruising around minding my own business one night and I got stopped by the police—just a routine stop, maybe one of my taillights is out or something—I would start thinking about that ticket, hoping the police person won't run my license through the computer. Of course the officer *would* run my license through the computer, it's standard procedure, and the word would come back that there was a warrant for my arrest for failure to pay that ticket. The next thing you know I'm in handcuffs and on my way to jail because of a speeding ticket. This has happened to me maybe four or five times in my life! Now let's take a look at the various points on the map of my personal experience that would clearly have shown me the difficulties waiting up the road. (This map might come in handy for you whenever you find yourself pushing that accelerator a little too close to the floor.)

First of all, there is already a warrant for my arrest for failing to pay an earlier ticket. Now here again I'm cruising too fast and there are signs that tell me so. They are the same signs that told me so the last time I was on this road. You know, the ones that say SPEED LIMIT 65. All of my life I've even seen other folks pulled over for going too fast. Back in high school, in

driver's education class, I learned that speeding could cause ac-
cidents and get you a ticket. But eighty-five feels nice. The car is
sailing smoothly. Stepping on the gas is easy. Piece of cake. No
problem. But oh-oh, here comes those flashing lights and that
guy in the Smokey the Bear hat and all of a sudden this fun and
exciting road has started to go uphill fast. It's too late to turn
around now. I failed to pay attention to the road signs all around
me. And I failed to look honestly at the map of my experience:
namely, the other times I had gotten tickets. So all I can do now
is pull over and wait for the inevitable. The officer walks up and
takes my license. He runs it through the computer. He writes
me a seventy- or eighty-dollar ticket and asks me to step out of
the car and assume the position. Right about now this easy road
is going straight up like the wall of a cliff. The road to the jail
isn't so hard. It's knowing I've been down this road before that's
rough. What's difficult is knowing that all I had to do was look
squarely at my map to see how hard the speeding road could
get. Or, how hard the road of not paying my earlier ticket would
become. If I had paid honest attention to my map I could have
avoided the hard road altogether. For sure I knew that if I got
caught speeding I'd get a ticket. I also knew that not paying a
ticket would result in a warrant for my arrest. I knew these
things in the back of my head, but I had let myself forget the
difficulties that a speeding ticket or not paying a ticket could
bring. I forgot about the embarrassment of being handcuffed on
the freeway with everybody watching. I forgot about the humiliation of riding in a police car with your hands locked behind

your back. I forgot about the jail guards making you take everything out of your pockets—taking your shoelaces and your belt
so you have to hold your pants up with your hand and flop
around in your shoes. I forgot about having to call a friend to
bring some money down to bail me out of jail. Because even
though I only owed seventy or eighty dollars for the ticket, now
I had to post several hundred dollars in bail to get out of jail just
to go to court later so I could pay the original seventy or eighty
bucks and explain to a judge why I didn't pay the ticket in the
first place. So I have to call on a friend for a favor. He loses time
from things he has to do. I lose time from work because of jail
and court. Not to mention the fine I have to pay in addition to
the cost of the tickets that I failed to pay in the first place. All of
these consequences, this difficult terrain and the landmarks
leading to it, were on my map. But I had let myself forget how
bad these areas are and how bad they made me feel. When you
feel as if you've been on a particular road before, just look at the
map of your own experience and be honest with yourself about
what you see. If it's your first time on a particular road, check
your baggage; there might be someone else's map in there that
will give you some indication of the difficulties that lie ahead.
(P.S. If you find yourself starting down this same road, look in
your bag. You may find the map of my experience, save yourself
a ticket, and/or a trip to jail.)

A map will show us the direction of a particular road. It
will also show us the condition of the road and landmarks along
the way. The exact location of large hills and mountains will be

evident when we look at the map. But in order to know what we will find along our journey we must not only look at the map but study it. Remember those charts I use when I'm preparing for a long flight in an airplane? I study those charts. They show me everything that lies on the ground along my path, including tall radio towers, towns, lakes, rivers, and mountains. They show me where I am in the air, whose airspace I'm flying in, and what other kinds of airplanes I should be looking out for. I don't fly without studying my maps because if I get lost in the air or I fly into restricted airspace I can't just pull over and ask directions. When I study my charts I feel confident the moment my plane lifts off the ground. Depending on the length of my flight, sometimes I have as many as four or five charts on the seat beside me. Together those charts tell me what lies along the path of my journey every step of the way. If I combine the information in them with my own observations as I am flying and with information gathered from other pilots and air-traffic controllers I significantly increase the odds of having a safe and successful flight. It's not what I see on the charts that makes me comfortable and confident. Sometimes what I see scares or intimidates me. But the information I receive from the charts allows me to make the right decision about how to fly over a high mountain range or across a vast expanse of desert. In fact, what I see on the charts may make me decide to avoid the mountains or the desert altogether and take another route on my journey. As a result, each time I fly I stand a better chance of staying alive, of enjoying the flight, and learning a little more about flying. As you walk toward manhood, the map of your own experience and the maps of others can help you stay alive, and teach you how to live. The map of our experience and the experience of others become roadmaps for our journeys if we "study" them.

We study the experiences of others in school all the time. It's called history class. But most of the time we only study the experiences of famous people or countries. We reflect on the experiences of nations and political and social groups. We study these people and their experiences, and the map of their experiences tells us things about the time period we're studying and people in general. But everyone makes a journey. And whether a man is considered famous or great makes little difference in determining the value of his journey. Even the experiences of men and women who are by most standards quite ordinary can become maps for our own journeys if we listen to their stories and examine them. It is the examination that will turn the experiences of average people just like ourselves into maps for our journey. If we're trying to get somewhere, when we get in the city it's good to know we have a bus or train schedule in our pocket. We can sit all day grinning about that schedule. But if we don't pull it out of our pocket, open it up, and examine it, we're going to have a hard time getting where we want to go. The map of experience is no different. We pull it out. We examine it, so that information can flow into our minds and our spirits and show us the way to make our journey.

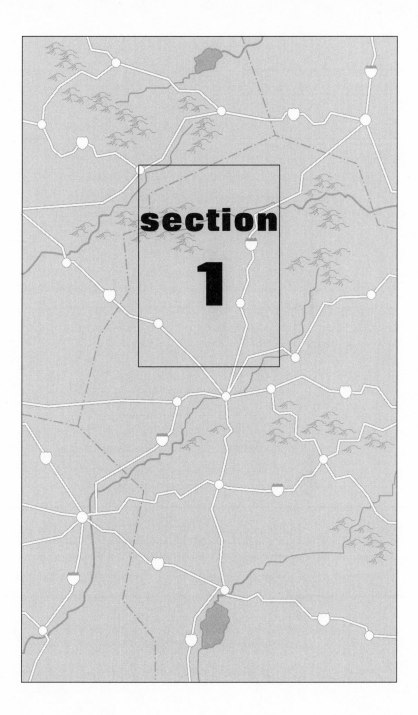

section

1

life

---

*I had to make my own living and
my own opportunity. . . . Don't sit down
and wait for the opportunities to come;
you have to get up and make them.*

—MADAME C. J. WALKER

My life is based as much on failure as on success. I have been told that along with success, failure and adversity form the rungs of a ladder that all men climb to good and useful lives. So it is with me. Even as I write these words I continue to fail and to fall. Some days, with luck, the wreckage of past failures forms a map on which I can clearly see, and perhaps even recognize, the lessons my current failure has to teach. Occasionally the signpost of a particular failure stays with me. Other times the signpost fades from my mind, and, almost inevitably, I take the wrong turn only to fail and fall once again. Then, just as before, failure forms a mental signpost on the map of my journey warning me and guiding me at the same time. The map of experience is just like a road map. You can carry it with you every mile of the journey, but if you fail to look at it, sooner or later you'll probably get lost.

Much of the wisdom in this book was discovered by honestly studying the map of my own journey and earnestly listening to the journeys of others. Today those folks and I happily share portions of the maps of our experience. We share our victories and our failures with you so that all our journeys may better lead us to good and useful lives.

Gentlemen, life is in session. Even when we're asleep life goes on. It never stops. Every day you and I must suit up and show up for life. Some days are harder than others. Some days are more fun than others. But we must show up. We will not always be successful when we show up. But one thing's for sure; if we don't suit up and show up there will be no success. There will be no win. Even if we win on Monday, Tuesday, and Wednesday we still have to show up the rest of the week. Because yesterday's score will not win today's ball game.

It's like this: The Bulls are going to play two games back to back. They come to the court and win on Saturday. When the Bulls come to the court on Sunday, instead of going to the hoop they sit on the bench in their street clothes for four quarters talking about Saturday's victory. If Jordan, Rodman, Pippen, and their teammates do this, no matter how good they are at B-ball the Bulls will lose Sunday's game. No matter how good yesterday's win was, no matter how much you talk about it, when there is a game to be played on Sunday, Saturday's game doesn't mean much. However, if the Bulls suit up and show up to shoot, rebound, and play defense as they did on Saturday, chances are they will be winners on Sunday too. Even if the opposing team plays well and the Bulls lose that Sunday game they can go home proud and confident that they played a hell of a game. You and I are not going to win every time we suit up. But we'll never win if we don't suit up and play. The showing up we did yesterday won't make us winners today. Yesterday's win might have helped us build our confidence and improve our skills, nonetheless you and I have got to take our confidence and our skills to the court every day in order to enjoy good and useful lives.

Showing up for life means every day is part of a journey—another long march toward the playoffs. However each boy's journey toward manhood is unique. No two paths are ever quite the same. What is similar about our journeys is that we need to suit up and show up every day.

I grew up without a father. My father's father died when

he was young and my father grew to manhood as best he could. Likewise, he left me to do the same. Perhaps since my father made it to adulthood without having a father, he came to believe a man was not needed to help mold a boy into a man. For a long time I believed that too.

I was reared in the Midwest by a loving mother who gave me the gift of the spoken and written word, and the gifts of music and good manners. Mom worked hard, often two or three jobs at a time. She had a friend named Joe, though most folks called him "Mr. Blue." Mr. Blue wasn't my dad, but he was all right with me. Mr. Blue taught me how to make a slingshot out of an old tire inner tube, hunt rabbits, fish, and stop a grounder. He wasn't always around, but the times we were together sure made a difference in my life. Maybe he's the reason some days I make my journey around Los Angeles on a candy apple–red motorcycle.

One day Mr. Blue brought over a bright red minibike for me to ride. It was a pretty thing. Store-bought with a three and a half horsepower Briggs and Stratton lawn-mower engine. The throttle was built right into the handlebars. The rear brake was operated by a chrome pedal just under the ball of the left foot. Mr. Blue had bought it for the Shriners' parade. Every Fourth of July he and his lodge brothers would put on clown suits and do figure eights up and down the parade route, their big Bozo shoes sticking out from the minibikes' footrests like wings.

"That thing's dangerous," Mom proclaimed the moment she saw the machine in the front yard.

"Ah, come on, Georgia," Mr. Blue moaned with a grin and wink to me. "It doesn't even go that fast."

My heart was in my throat. Twisting the throttle all the way and zooming down the gravel alley beside our house meant more to me at that moment than anything else in the world. It was as if the unmuffled puttering of the engine and the feel of the bike between my legs were the only things that would ever matter! I followed the debate intently. As the words pushed and pulled between them it seemed that Mr. Blue's arguments were losing ground. He just wasn't making a strong enough case for my being allowed to ride that minibike! He left me no choice but to speak on my own behalf.

"I won't ride it in the street, Momma, just up and down the alley. And . . . and . . . Mr. Blue is right too. It really doesn't go that fast. It just looks like it goes fast 'cause it's real small."

Momma frowned. "Boy, be quiet. You don't even know how to ride that thing."

"Uh huh! Andy Wills's cousin had one, and he let me ride it. He showed me!"

Mom squeezed her lips together and ignored me. "Well, I'm tellin' ya," she went on, disgusted, "those things are dangerous. People get hurt on 'em all the time."

Momma turned around as she said this and headed for the kitchen, still prophesying disaster. Mr. Blue and I looked at each other, expressionless. She hadn't said yes, but she hadn't said no either. We had won! I grinned at Mr. Blue. He grinned back and winked again. I bolted for the bike, banging the wooden screen door open with the palm of my hand. I jumped down the short set of red brick steps and landed on my feet in the dirt next to the minibike. Mr. Blue followed, easing toward the screen door in long exaggerated strides on his heels while looking back over his shoulder toward the kitchen. He escaped out of the front door, grabbed the gas can, and quickly filled the minibike's tank. I steadied myself and pulled the starter cord. Once, twice, three times. Nothing. Mr. Blue adjusted the choke and turned the throttle a couple times. I pulled again and the engine sputtered into action. It was time. Mr. Blue nodded to me to mount the machine.

"Don't go too fast now," he warned. "Take it easy. Keep your foot on the brake."

I nodded respectfully, slowly twisting the throttle toward me, and the bike began to move. Slowly at first, then steadily picking up speed. I tried my best to maintain a serious, safety-conscious expression, but my face quickly gave way to a huge grin as I wobbled forward for the first few yards. Confidence came quickly. Continuing down the unpaved dirt path in front of my house I forgot about the foot brake and as I approached the corner I put my feet down to stop. Fortunately, my hand remembered the brake on the handlebars just before I leapt the curb into the street. By the time I had tooled up and down the path a couple of times a crowd of envious, eager boys had gathered at the corner of Cleveland and Hutton.

"Where you get the minibike, man?" Steve Tate asked.

"My dad," I said, on the move and out of earshot of Mr. Blue. Even though Mr. Blue didn't live with me and Mom, most of the neighborhood kids didn't know that he wasn't really my dad. Mr. Blue had been around since I could remember. I really couldn't think of anything else to call him. Although I never risked calling him Dad or referring to him as my father to others when he was around, it was the easiest way for me to define our relationship. Both to myself and to others.

"How fast do it go?" somebody asked.

"Prob'ly thirty or forty, I bet," assured a second kid.

"No way," came a voice from the crowd.

"Bet!" challenged the second kid.

"How much?" replied the doubter.

"A dollar."

"Man, you must be crazy. I ain't bettin' you no dollar. How fast do it go, boy?" demanded the doubter.

"You see a boy, spit on him," I replied, backing the minibike up and away from the center of the crowd.

"I got your boy, punk. How fast do it go?" the doubter demanded again, knifing his way toward me through the crowd. I was relieved to see he was smiling.

"I dunno. 'Bout twenty or thirty, I guess."

"See I told you, punk," the doubter exclaimed, triumphant. "That thing don't go no forty or fifty."

While the other boys chimed in offering their estimate of

the minibike's maximum speed I turned the mechanical wonder around and zoomed the seventy or eighty yards back toward Mr. Blue, opening up the throttle all the way. For the first time in my life I was the envy of the neighborhood boys, if only for a few minutes. I was so grateful for that minibike. I was so grateful for Mr. Blue.

Mr. Blue was a professional house painter. In addition to houses, for more than twenty years he painted the walls, halls, exterior trim, and yellow lines in the parking lot of a local hospital. Sometimes I would get to stop by the hospital for a visit. A visit to Mr. Blue's job meant a visit to the hospital's boiler room and a chance to hang around real workin' men in sawdust-covered overalls and paint-speckled work pants. Men with thin mustaches, girlie calendars, and dirty jokes. Guys with dry hands and knotty knuckles, who kept a bottle of scotch or a six-pack in the trunk of the car at all times. At their coffee break in the boiler room they sat on gray wooden benches, munched on snacks brought from home, and sipped steaming hot coffee from scratched aluminum thermoses. I stood nearby, quietly waiting for Mr. Blue to return from his job site somewhere in the building. "You seen Blue?" one workman would ask another, noticing me trying to remain unnoticed.

"Naw. He's been workin' over on the west wing all morning."

"He know you were comin'?" the workman asked me, hunched over and cradling the hot cup in both hands. His lips barely touched the cup's rim, and I could hear the sound of too-hot coffee being sucked into his mouth.

"I guess so." My shoulders shrugged.

"You're his boy, ain't ya?" A lanky young workman with a long chin and an overbite reminded the room.

My head nodded the lie. But before my mind could take it back I remembered the couple of times somebody had asked Mr. Blue if I was "his boy" and how he had smiled and replied, "Yeah," without so much as a pause.

"Go on over and see if he's still there," an older workman ordered with an upward jerk of his head and a downward flick of his Pall Mall cigarette.

With one workman's permission and another's directions I traveled the hospital halls until I found Mr. Blue. More than once, after I had found him, I'd ask why it was every time I came to the hospital he was painting the same room. He'd laugh and deny it and assure me that it was not the same room but only that most of the rooms looked the same. Then I'd laugh and double check my senses. Many years later it occurred to me that over the course of twenty years a hospital room or hallway might require several coats of paint, and that on some of those visits, stretched over many years, Mr. Blue was indeed painting the same room I had seen him paint on other days in other years. In a sense, my boyhood could be measured by the coats of paint on those county hospital walls. Or by the number of brush and roller strokes registered deep in the muscles of Mr. Blue's hands and arms. Mr. Blue had strong hands with big veins and long, bony fingers. It was those hands that I was counting on to lead me on my journey from the land of boys to the land of men.

When I was fourteen my journey took me to a boarding school in a neighboring state. That was the same year that Mom and Mr. Blue started to argue somewhat regularly. I hardly knew any of the details; I was away at school. Besides, at fourteen what went on between adults was ''grown folks'' business, business that kids were supposed to stay out of.

From where I sit at this moment of my journey—through years of distance—I can see Mr. Blue far more clearly now than then. I sense his love for my mother. His fear of expressing that love. And his fear of losing the love she had given. I understand now that Mr. Blue may have been unable to accept the truth that women too are on a journey. That like men, women must be free to choose their own destinations. I believe that it was Mr. Blue's unwillingness to accept this truth about my mother which brought all three of us to the summer night I woke to find my mother bleeding on the sofa from a gunshot wound. Mom lived. Both she and Mr. Blue said it was an accident. And I was grateful to have that to believe. Yet, because he had hurt my mother I could never again bring myself to fully trust Mr. Blue as my guide into the world of men. If, as a man, he had found it necessary to point a gun at my mother while she lay resting, let alone pull the trigger, then how accurate could his map of the land of men be?

Ultimately, I chose to journey toward manhood on my

own. I had no father, and Mr. Blue was unable to be my sponsor. Consequently, I took lots of wrong turns. Many times I
became confused about the world of men. I mistook the world
of men for a world where a man's worth was measured primarily in relation to women, wealth, and war. I came to believe that
my popularity among women, lots of money in my pocket, and
my success in competition with other men was the mark of
manhood. These misconceptions got me lost sometimes and led
me to obstacles that were often difficult to overcome. Some of
those obstacles were of my own making; some had been built by
others. What was similar about those obstacles was that regard-
less of who had built them it was me who had to climb over,
under, or around them.

Gentlemen, the journey is mine. No matter where an obstacle comes from or who constructed the doggone thing it's me
who has to get past that obstacle. I'm the one who has to suit
up, show up, and get on with my journey. I may not be responsible for the problem, but I must be responsible for the solution.
Actually, winning has very little to do with other people. Who
we're really playing against is ourselves. Our own shortcoming
and fears. If we can beat those things in us, we'll be winners. I
am the result of many chefs who added a unique blend of ingre-
dients to the stew that I am: my mother, teachers, friends,
books, songs, television, the church, Mr. Blue. As a result of
those varying blends I am not solely responsible for the kind of
young man I became. Some of the chefs who helped prepare me
made mistakes. Others deliberately put bitter and hurtful herbs

into the pot. Still others placed in my pot the sweetest fruit imaginable. But whatever their contributions, here I am. What is right with me is right. What is wrong is wrong. But what is wrong can, perhaps, be corrected. I may need help "fixing me," but I *must* be responsible for making sure that what is wrong gets right.

warriors

---

*The battles that count aren't the ones
for gold medals. The struggles
within yourself—the invisible, inevitable
battles inside all of us—that's where it's at.*

—JESSE OWENS

I used to watch lots of war movies when I was younger. Loved 'em. The action was great. But what I liked most about those war movies was how the guys really came to care about one another. It always seemed that the guy you least expected would be the one to do something really great, really heroic. That was often the guy who died saving his buddies. I always thought I'd like to go out like that: in a war, earning the respect of my friends and fellow soldiers; caring so much about somebody else and having so much courage that I'd lay down my life for them. A lot of what I learned about being a man I got from those war movies. For a long time it seemed to me that the mark of a real man was how he died.

After my freshman year of college I joined the Marines. The Vietnam War wasn't quite over and I was worried I'd miss the war of my generation. From the time I was a young kid I had watched America's opposition to the war grow. By the time I was old enough to serve it was clear to me that America was fed up with war, and that it would be a long time before another came along. By then I was sure I'd be too old to go; so I left college and joined up. I never went into combat. The war ended a few months after I enlisted. I never got to grab a machine gun, kill a bunch of guys I didn't know, and save my platoon. I never got the chance to fall on a grenade and sacrifice myself for a good buddy. And thank God I never had the chance to find out I was nowhere near as brave as I'd always hoped I'd be.

For years after I left the Marines I was ashamed that I'd never gone to war and had no stories of horror or heroism to tell. But today, the more I suit up and show up for this thing we've been talking about called "Life," the more I realize that when you set living and dying side by side, dying is probably the easier thing to do. I can't be completely sure this is true because I've never tried dying (well, that's not exactly the truth either, but we'll talk more about that later). But it seems to me that death happens only once. You die and no matter how difficult that dying is you only have to go through it once. Even if death is some big bony guy in a black hooded outfit riding around on a horse and carrying a sickle, you only have to meet that ugly sucker once. Life, on the other hand, keeps popping up day after day, night after night. And unless we have a premature showdown with Mr. Death we have to keep meeting Mr. Life over and over again.

If we keep suiting up and showing up for life there's no question that some days are going to be pretty rough. Some situations, as you well know, can get downright ugly. Maybe even as ugly as death. But we need to show up anyhow. We need to walk through it. We journey on. The ugly days will pass, sooner or later, to better days. Think about it. Think about all the things that had you upset or worried last week, or last month. How many of those things still have you upset or worried? Sure there's some leftover stuff that keeps you hangin', but a lot of it has passed on. It's not buggin' you anymore. Just look at your own life, and you'll know what I'm talking about. Eventually a lot of the ugly stuff passes. When we're surrounded by ugly days that never seem to pass, it might be that we're stuck on our journey and need to call for help. It's sort of like running off the road into a ditch; we probably need to call a tow truck or some friends to help push or pull us out. Remember, no man has to travel alone. A man who asks for help is still a man, and probably a better man for the asking.

Surviving the day-to-day mess, that's the hard part! That's what makes a true warrior. A solid, daily goal for us is not to let the hard, ugly days take us out.

I know a guy named Ray. His son, Brian, has brain cancer.

For the last several years Brian has been in and out of hospitals and has had surgery dozens of times. Most of those times Ray has been with him. Brian's a pretty average kid. He likes "Baywatch" and video games, and takes karate lessons. Ray doesn't baby Brian because he's sick. I've seen him give his son that "you know better" look out of the corner of his eye when Brian was just a few hours out of surgery. Ray talks with his son about the realities of his illness and the probability of death. Ray plays with his son and hugs him too. Some days Brian is in a lot of pain and that means Ray is in a lot of pain too. There are nights when Ray can't be sure if Brian is going to wake up the next morning. But Ray keeps suiting up and showing up no matter what.

In spite of his son's pain, in spite of his own pain, Ray continues to show up for life. And so does Brian. Ray and Brian are warriors. Each day they make a journey and confront obstacles: sickness and fear. Brian's sickness is like a huge mountain in their path. The mountain is so high and so wide that neither Ray nor Brian can see what lies ahead. On some days the mountain casts a long dark shadow over their journey. That mountain of sickness is real and perhaps even insurmountable. Each day, like mountaineers, Ray and Brian climb the mountain of sickness that lies in their path. They have to climb it because they can't move it. They must climb that mountain because in fact the mountain is no longer just an obstacle that blocks their path, the mountain is the path itself. Right now there is no cure for pediatric brain cancer. So Ray and Brian climb because they must.

Climbing the mountain is what they are supposed to do! Remember, *life is in session* gentlemen! This means our daily session of life will sometimes see us moving straight ahead, and other times our journey will take us up the side of a mountain whose walls are as steep as a downtown office building: Life is like that sometimes. Some days Ray and Brian make more progress up the mountain than on others. I imagine that just as there must be scary moments for mountain climbers there are scary moments for Ray, maybe when Brian is in surgery and he can't be sure exactly how things are going to come out. For Brian I guess it must be scary sitting in a hospital bed waiting to see if the surgery will make him better. But it's all part of their journey—the fear, the worry, and the waiting: it's all climbing.

Ray and Brian's *fear* is a different kind of obstacle. It's more like a thick, muddy road that could keep them stuck at the base of the mountain. The mud threatens to keep them from putting one foot in front of the other and making the difficult journey up the slope. Too many of us succumb to the fear that keeps us from climbing, the fear that keeps us from suiting up and showing up the fear that comes from somewhere in our heads. In fact, it may be that our fear is in our feet! You see, for a warrior the battle is not only with the mountain but with his feet. Warriors like Ray and Brian must make their feet move in order to climb the mountain. And in order to do that they must conquer that muddy road. As warriors we must face our fear so that we can move our feet and climb the mountains that so very often become part of our journey.

Ray is no doctor. He can't make his son well. Many days are not winning days for Ray and Brian but they both keep showing up anyhow. Because there are good days too. Lots of them. Great days in fact. Days when Brian gets to ride on the back of a motorcycle or reach level twelve on his favorite video game. The good days and the bad days are what make the journey that Ray and Brian travel good and useful. And their lives have been useful to thousands of people around the world. Because Ray and Brian have been willing to share the map of their journeys, the good days and the bad, dozens of doctors and researchers are racing toward finding a cure for the kind of brain cancer that affects kids. Every year all over the country folks like Jay Leno and thousands of other motorcyclists get together and ride their bikes to raise money to fund the research that helps kids like Brian. I received a call some months ago from a friend in New Jersey. One of his employee's children had just been diagnosed with brain cancer, he told me. I called Ray and Ray immediately called that child's father. Ray shared the map of his experience with that father. Of course that father in New Jersey has to make his own climb with his own sick child. But perhaps because of Ray's experience on the climb, the New Jersey father will know a little more about the mountain—footholds and handholds and places to rest along the way. Perhaps, thanks to Ray, the warriors from New Jersey will understand that on some days their path will be the mountain. And that to climb the mountain the warrior must first focus on his feet.

The mountain, the obstacle, can be the path itself. Often

obstacles form a section of the road we must travel on our journey. But why climb? Why struggle up the mountain when it would be easier to stay at the mountain's base and accept the dark shadow it casts over our lives? The reason we climb is because so much of our strength, our wisdom, and our manhood lies up the side of that mountain. Long distance Tanzanian runners prepare themselves for a race by running up the side of Mount Kilimanjaro, one of the world's tallest mountains. As they make their way up the mountain the African runners grow stronger. Their endurance builds. Their confidence increases. Even if they fall or stop to rest, their strength grows because the runner's growth, like our own growth, comes not with speed or reaching the mountain's peak but with the effort he puts into every stride. Sure the going is tough. But there is a saying that "what doesn't kill you makes you stronger." For a warrior it is the mountain that makes him stronger and wiser. Each stride we take on our journey up the mountain of adversity and pain will, if it does not kill us, make us better warriors.

There is no need to go out and look for a mountain so you can grow to be a better warrior. There is no need to create obstacles, adversity, and pain for yourself or others. As long as you keep suiting up and showing up, trust me, the mountains will find you. One thing about mountain climbers though, they usually work in teams, looking out for one another as they go. When you find yourself headed up a mountain, look below you. There may be another warrior trying to make his way up too. Reach back and give him a hand. Pull him up to you. Perhaps the two of you can climb side by side and do some good lookin' out. Look above you too. There might be somebody up above reaching a hand down to help you up. There might be another warrior up there throwing down a rope to help you keep from falling. To help keep a hard day's climb from taking you out.

honor

If a man can reach the latter days
of his life with his soul intact,
he has mastered life.

—GORDON PARKS

Now I don't want you to think I was all that anxious to die on the battlefield. I'm not crazy. But it seemed to me that being a soldier—a great warrior—was a pretty direct way of earning the respect of others. And based on the movies I had seen, it was a very good way to get a woman, a sharp uniform, and a few medals. Courage under fire—girls seemed to love that sort of thing. And so did guys. Even moms and dads were proud to have a brave son in uniform. In all the war movies I watched men never said a lot to each other about how they felt and what they were afraid of, but there was always this thing about

"Honor." It wasn't talked about, but it was there. You could feel it jump out at you from the television screen. In these movies, if you fought hard and fearlessly and managed to stay alive through it all, you became a man of honor. If you faced the enemy bravely and died under fire, you were a man of honor. If you were captured, starved, and beaten, but you kept your mouth shut, you were an honorable guy. Alive or dead, honor was the reward. The brave and fearless guys in the movies were men of honor. No doubt about it, I wanted to be a man of honor too. I wanted the love and respect of the people in my neighborhood and the girls at school. I wanted the men in my community to think of me as a man. I wanted my mother to be proud of me.

Honor is a fine thing. Having a reputation as a man of honor is an extremely valuable asset. Shakespeare wrote: "Who steals my purse steals trash. . . . But he that filches from me my good name . . . makes me poor indeed." In other words, a guy can steal my wallet and it isn't that big a deal. I can get another wallet and some more money too. But if a guy starts messing around with my honor and my reputation, both he and I have a serious problem. When I was young my mother used to tell me "a man's word is his bond." Unfortunately, she never explained to me just what that saying meant. When I would ask her to explain it she would say, "Common sense ought to tell you what it means." Too often, it seems, common sense failed to tell me what it was telling everybody else. It took me a long while to understand not only that saying, but the true meaning of honor as well.

For a lot of my adult years I continued to think of honor in terms of what other people thought about me. If you asked me to write a paragraph telling what kind of person I was, I probably would have felt more comfortable asking a friend to do the writing. What others thought of me was more important to me than what I thought of myself. As a result, my definition of what was truly honorable was also determined by other people. If my idea of an honorable response to a problem was different from my friends', I would probably abandon my response. I would wait until I found out how my friends were going to respond. It didn't matter what I felt deep inside. I took the group's decision to be the honorable one, and hid my natural, initial response in the back of my mind.

When I was a Marine recruit I got up one night and helped a bunch of other recruits beat the living daylights out of a guy. Our rationale was, he wasn't one of us. He didn't fit in. He wasn't turning out to be a good warrior. So, we figured if we beat him up it might get him in line. Inside, I knew that thirty guys jumping on one guy was not the honorable thing to do. But in the Marine Corps, beatings like this were called blanket parties, and blanket parties were, I was told, an age-old tradition in the Corps. Among some Marines a blanket party was considered an honorable act. But there was never any doubt in *my* mind, before, during, or after the beating that thirty guys covering one guy with blankets and punching him was cowardly and wrong and therefore not honorable. So, why did I go along? Because I accepted twenty-nine other guys' definition of honor.

And maybe they did it because they also accepted twenty-nine other guys' definition of honor. What's weird is that if just one of us had held to our own concept of honor and said: "Hey, you guys, I don't think this is an honorable thing"—if one of us had spoken up—it might have spared one guy a lot of pain. And it certainly would have spared me a lot of guilt, because for years afterward I was ashamed of what I did that night. Even as I participated in the beating I knew that it was wrong but I failed to speak up because I was afraid. Why was I afraid? I wasn't scared that the other recruits would beat me up. No, I was afraid they might stop seeing me as one of the guys. I feared that they might laugh and make fun of me the way we did to the guy we had beaten. If I didn't go along I feared I would be viewed as a man without honor. The funny thing is, by going along with the fellas, I remained an honorable guy to them but not to myself. Over the years I betrayed my own sense of honor a lot, so much so that some days it was hard for me to look in the mirror. In fact, for a long time I tried to get as far away from myself as possible because nobody, not even me, wanted a dishonorable man around.

Many of you guys are challenged in the same way on your journeys. One group tells you to do this, wear that. The other says do that, wear this. We have people telling us who to hate, who to love, and who's not fit to live. It's even harder to stand up for your honor when people are threatening to hurt you if you don't do as they say to do, or think as they say to think.

Somewhere out there, however, maybe near or maybe far, there are others who share your sense of honor. Find them. Search them out. It might be one of your "boys." Maybe a teacher, a coach, your mother or father or grandparent. It might be some strangers you read about in the paper or hear about on the news. People who just kick it in an honorable way. People suiting up and showing up for life instead of death. People showing up to make things better instead of worse. Sometimes it's hard to hang on to your honor all by yourself. Get help. Ask for help. Go find help.

I was at a dance once sitting over in a corner with a bunch of other guys, frontin'—trying to be cool. The beat was pushing through the soles of my shoes and up into my knees. I wanted to dance and have a good time but I didn't know any of the ladies there and I was kind of scared to ask somebody. So I just hung out in the corner with a bunch of other guys who were holding up the walls. Finally this brother I had seen around a few times strolled over to me and said, "Yo, homey. You got to come to the party. The party ain't gonna come to you."

At first I was mad because he had peeped my stuff. But then I had to smile 'cause I knew he was right. I was sitting over in the corner (next to the fellas, but really all by myself), scared to dance, frontin' like everything was cool but really wanting to be out there with the people who were moving to the kind of music I loved to move to. After a few minutes I got up and went over and stood in the middle of a small crowd at the edge of the dance floor. Everybody was rockin' in place. I got to rockin' too. Some girl in the crowd saw that I needed to rock and nodded toward the dance floor. I could tell that we shared the same sense of rhythm. I could tell by the way she smiled that we both believed that the funk was an honorable groove. A moment later we started to dance.

When we're uncomfortable with what we are doing and where we are, we need to get up, join the party, and get comfortable. This can be hard because sometimes finding out where we belong, getting up and going to our kind of party, can mean leaving people behind: people we love and care for, people who love us, people who look like us, talk like us and dance like us.

The thing to remember is, a lot of the reason why the thought of leaving our corner and going across the way is frightening is because the corner where we are sitting, no matter how uncomfortable it is, is a familiar corner. A safe corner. So there we are, sitting in this corner, surrounded by this bunch of people, and uncomfortable—because the folks around us are about the kind of thing we're not. But if across the way is where people who share your idea of honor are hanging out, then that's where you need to be because it's hard holding on to your groove, your sense of honor, all by yourself, especially when you're surrounded by folks whose idea of honor is vastly different from yours. We all want to be respected among our peers.

Every man wants to be thought of as a stand-up guy. This is why it can be so easy to betray our sense of honor when we feel the need to belong. The basic human need to be respected among one's peers can be so great that we sacrifice our honor for the sake of love and belonging. And needing to belong is okay. You do belong. It's finding out *where* you belong that is one of your journey's destinations. In fact it's many destinations. Each man, if he chooses, can belong in many different places and with many different kinds of people. We can be comfortable in all of these places as long as we can stay true to what we believe in. As long as we are able to be part of people and places and still maintain our groove, our personal standard of honor, we can belong in a million wonderful places across the galaxy.

anger

---

*You must be willing to suffer the anger
of the opponent, and yet not return anger.
No matter how emotional your opponents
are, you must remain calm.*

—MARTIN LUTHER KING, JR.

If your fuse is short like mine you know that we can "go off" in
a heartbeat. The thing we don't often realize is that when we go
off, it hurts people something awful. The thing is, we're probably pretty nice guys. People generally like us. We're fun. We
have a good sense of humor, and we're fairly smart. Our anger,
when we unleash it, is 180 degrees from the person we usually
are. Our angry person scares people to death. And they think
we're a little crazy because we can be so very different in such a
short period of time. We're sort of like Dr. Jekyll and Mr. Hyde.

It doesn't usually seem that way to us, but through others' eyes our anger is scary. When you and I go off, people's ears shut down. They may still be looking at us but they've stopped listening. They may just walk away in their minds. Or they may be on guard, ready to defend themselves against our words or what they fear we might do next. Whatever, they've stopped listening to us. And when people can't hear what you're trying to tell them, your journey can become very difficult indeed. I've gone off on people I've employed because I believed that they had not done properly the work I was paying them to do. After I went off I was satisfied that they had "gotten the message." Much to my surprise, a few days later the same problem would resurface, and I would go off again. "Don't you understand what I'm saying, fool! I want it done such and such a way! Now do it or I'll get someone who can!"

Almost inevitably, a little while later here it comes again. Maybe not quite as bad as the last time but still not the way I'd asked for the work to be done. Of course not. How could the job get done any better when the person I'm speaking to is only hearing the tone of my voice and not the content of my conversation? Almost always when I hold my anger, stay calm, and speak in a moderate voice my requests are heard. And if the person is truly capable of doing a better job then the job gets done properly.

Our temper hurts people's feelings too. We're so nice most of the time, then—Wham!—off we go. They just don't know how to take it. Sometimes it's the bad days that make us want to do and say stupid stuff. But often the negative way we respond to a difficult day compounds the day's ugliness and causes that ugliness to grow into a monster whose greatest danger is to ourselves.

For instance, imagine you're walking home from school and you're confronted by a thing from outer space. You know, big, ugly, lots of teeth with spit dripping from its mouth. From the way the thing looks, it appears that it does not have your best interests at heart. The situation, then, is clear: in order for you to get home you're going to have to deal with this monster right now. The first thing you think of is your Monster Popper, which is in your backpack. So, you pull it out, point it at the spit-dripping thing ahead of you, and—*pop!*—you blast away. But instead of rolling over dead or running away, the monster multiplies ten times right in front of your eyes. No problem. You pop it again, with a vengeance.

This time, however, it multiplies ten, twenty, thirty times! And now, instead of one monster you're dealing with a whole army of monsters who will almost certainly eat you alive. What caused this situation to worsen? What made the problem bigger than it was in the first place? Of course, it was our response to the problem. Perhaps we should have considered our options more carefully before we attacked. Perhaps we should have asked the monster why it was in the neighborhood before we reached for the ol' Monster Popper. Sure the monster *looked* ugly and dangerous, but was it really going to hurt us? And further, even though it looked dangerous, did the monster really have the *power* to hurt us?

It's often the same with people and real life situations. Often, when I fail to pause before I act, I make things worse. Someone says something to me that sounds ugly. They say something that hurts my feelings. It may even be a legitimate criticism spoken to help me be better than I am. But then I go off—curse, yell, or maybe even get ready to fight; and what happens? The other person sees a monster in front of them. A screaming, yelling, face-twisted-all-up ugly monster cursing and showing its claws. So, what do they do? They get on the defensive, quick! They might not stop to think their words have hurt us, or that we have mistaken their criticism as a put-down. What they know is the situation looks ugly. So they get really ugly and the next thing you know we both have our poppers out and the hurting is almost certainly going to worsen on both sides. Most people call this "escalation."

This kind of "escalation" used to happen between me and my teachers in high school. A teacher would say something to me that sounded ugly, usually a comment about my schoolwork or my behavior. Of course I would go off and find myself a short time later in the vice principal's office. Just that quick, what seemed like a bad situation had gotten worse. Now let's take a closer look:

The teacher's job is to teach. So a teacher has every

right to comment on my performance and/or my behavior in class—it's part of the job. It's also part of the teacher's job to critique my schoolwork, and if that work is not cool, a teacher is supposed to tell me about it. Now, hopefully, my teacher is respectful and tells me what is wrong with my assignment in a courteous manner. But maybe not. Teachers are people too, and they're not always perfect. But one thing's certain: if I come back at that teacher in a disrespectful manner, disrespect is what will come back at me, disrespect and discipline.

Even if a person comes to me disrespectfully, I need to stay calm and consider the situation. An aggressive, disrespectful response on my part can severely worsen the situation. Especially in an environment where I am not in charge of my journey, like school. In school, teachers are part of the journey. So, a teacher comes to me about my journey, but he comes to me with an attitude. Sure I can go off and demand that the teacher give me respect. But only two things are likely to happen. (1) The teacher's attitude will get thicker. (2) The teacher may choose to remind me who is currently running my journey by disciplining me. I can get an attitude, but the result is the same. I lose: detention, suspension, expulsion.

The teacher continues on her journey; she goes right on teaching. But it is now more difficult for me to continue on my journey, which is learning. It may not be fair, but that's part of the journey. It is real life. Remember, Life Is In Session. If my response to my teacher had been calm, my teacher would have had little power to interrupt my journey. When I go off on people I give them the power to interrupt my journey. It's a fact of life that without my cooperation it is much more difficult for people to interfere with my journey.

fear

The brave man carves out his fortune,
and every man is the son of his own works.
—MIGUEL DE CERVANTES

Fear is a natural instinct we've all been given to help keep us safe. At birth we all received just the right dose. But sometimes as we travel on our journey we get many more doses of fear than we need. And too much fear is unhealthy.

Throughout my life fear has been a lot like fire. Some days fear has kept me safe. Like a wall of fire in my mind, fear has kept me from stepping into certain catastrophe. Other days that same fire wall of fear has appeared in my mind and the sight of it has paralyzed me and prevented me from suiting up and showing up for life. Fear will keep you from jumping into the lion compound at the zoo—and in so doing, fear will save your life. Fear can also keep you from jumping into new experiences and new ways of thinking. Fear has prevented me from meeting and talking to people I really wanted to talk to. I was afraid they would not like me. As a student, fear of failure sometimes made me shy away from challenging courses. "What if I fail?" I thought. My fear of what might happen by the end of the semester kept me from doing what I needed to do at the beginning of the semester!

When I was fourteen my mother and I started talking about college. "You know I probably can't afford to send you," she said sitting atop her stool at the kitchen counter.

"Yeah, I know."

"So how are you gonna' get through college, do you think?" Mom asked. Of course she already knew the answer. But a lot of times Georgia would just ask me something to see if *I* knew the answer.

"I'll get a scholarship," I replied. Not really paying too much attention.

"How you gonna do that?"

She was about to get on my nerves now. Because she knew full well that was a question I had absolutely no answer to at all. As far as I was concerned, college was a long way off. And at the age of fourteen I wasn't in the habit of looking that far ahead on my journey.

A few months later Mother presented me with an entry

TOLLESTON

form for the local Optimist International Oratorical Contest. According to the instructions, all participants were to write a speech no more than five minutes in length and then deliver that speech before a panel of judges. The prize was a five-hundred-dollar scholarship and a chance to compete on the state and national level for even more scholarship money. "I think you should enter," Mother said, without looking up from the evening paper.

"How am I gonna write a speech?" I asked sincerely.

"Just sit down and write it," she replied from behind the paper.

"How am I going to 'just sit down and write it'?" I asked in disbelief.

Mother lowered the paper to her lap and smiled. "I don't know. Just sit down somewhere and write it."

That was it. The smile made me lose it. That and the fact that she was telling me to do something, and *she* couldn't even tell me how!

"I'm not writin' no stupid speech," I announced, risking raising my voice a bit. "I don't know how. Why do you always want to make me do something I don't know how to do?" I inquired angrily.

"I'm not trying to make you do anything. I'm simply suggesting that you enter the contest because the prize is a scholarship."

"Sure," I smirked. "Five hundred dollars. How am I going to go to college on five hundred dollars?"

"I'm not suggesting you go to college on five hundred dollars. All I said was, I think you should enter the contest."

It was clear that it was time for me to shut up. Mother's speech had started to get very perfect. I mean her lips had gotten tight and she was overenunciating her words. These were sure signs that her patience and my margin of safety were growing thin. I retreated angry but silent to my private place in the basement. Occasionally over the next few weeks Mom would ask me if I had completed the entry form. Each time I said no she simply looked at me for a moment then went on about what she was doing.

"When are you going to get that form filled out?" Mom asked flatly for the umpteenth time.

"What form?"

"Boy, don't be stupid. You know what form. The form for the oratorical contest. The deadline is fast approaching."

With that phrase "fast approaching" she had jumped dead on my nerves, with both feet. She was always talking like that, all formal and stuff: "fast approaching." Who talks like that? "Quick get out of the way! The car is 'fast approaching!' " The fact is she was mad. She always spoke like that when she was mad.

"Aw, come on, Mom," I pleaded. "I can't write. . . ."

"Well, you will," Georgia commanded. "Get it filled out so you can send it in."

Mom had waited nearly a month for me to see the light on my own and enter that contest. Finally she made the decision for me.

By the time I mailed the entry form the contest was only two weeks away. The topic for that year was "Youth, Full Partners in a Better Tomorrow." Every evening I sat at the kitchen table and Mom sat on her stool at the counter. I had picked up a book on speech writing at the library. The first thing you should do, the book said, is to make an outline of the primary points you want to make. The first couple of nights were the worst. I had no idea what my primary points should be. I remember Mom giving me a kick start by asking me some questions about what it meant to be a partner, and what kind of qualities a person needed to help make a better tomorrow. By the end of the first week I had started to write and even to rewrite a little. After composing a paragraph or two I'd read it to her. "How's that sound?" I'd ask.

"Umm, not too bad." Then she might zero in on a particular word or phrase I had used and suggest that maybe I could find a word that better fit what I was trying to say. It was during the writing of that first speech that I discovered an incredible tool called a thesaurus. At fourteen my vocabulary was a little limited when it came to writing about adult topics. But inside the thesaurus I could always find just the right word, mostly new words, to help me say exactly what I wanted to say.

For several days I worked well into the evening, often falling asleep at the table only to have Mom wake me up and say, "Read that last bit to me again," or "What word did you find?" "Do you think that works a little better?" This went on every weekday evening and weekend afternoon until the day before the contest. If there hadn't been someone there to push me toward writing that speech you can be sure I never would have written a word.

Nobody likes to lose and look bad, and I'm no exception, and before that first speech I didn't know anything about writing speeches. But I did know that because I knew nothing about the subject it would be hard work. I also knew that since it was my first time it probably wouldn't be a very good speech. "At least not good enough to win that scholarship," I had reasoned. This fear of difficult work, losing, and looking bad nearly kept me from learning a skill that is enabling me to write this chapter, right now. This morning when I started writing the story about that first oratorical contest I had absolutely no fear of putting my thoughts on paper. I've done it so many times now. The thesaurus is behind me on the shelf. I've written so many speeches, essays, plays, and now a couple of books that I'm not afraid anymore. I know I can do it. Sometimes I get scared wondering if anyone will want to hear or read what I've written. Will people like it? Will it have meaning for them? Yet more than a few times now, I've written things and shared them with others and some liked what I wrote, while others did not. But there was always at least one person who believed that what I had to say was worth listening to. Sometimes when I write I think of that one person and my fear goes away a little. Other times I have to call myself back from tomorrow and the question of whether or not other folks will like what I've written. I actually have to call out loud to myself "Hey, Greg, come back! Come back! Stay in the now!"

The now is this moment and this laptop computer. I know that I can put words on this screen. I'm doing it right now and there is very little fear in it. So I stay in this moment and it helps me stay out of the fear. Even when there is fear in this moment, it's usually no more than I can handle. But when I add the fear that comes with what may or may not happen tomorrow it often weighs me down so badly that I am unable to focus on today.

I came in second in that contest. Some other kid won the scholarship money. But by the time I graduated from high school I had earned nearly a full scholarship to a small college in my home state as a member of the speech team. As a member of the team I was able to compete nationally as an orator, writing speeches and delivering them before a panel of judges.

Before that first writing I was paralyzed by fear. I needed money for college but fear almost kept me from getting the money I needed. Fortunately, my mother was with me on that part of my journey to help me climb over that obstacle—to walk through that fire wall of fear. A lot of times when fear keeps us from showing up, suiting up, and moving forward in life we need others to drag us kicking and screaming up the road. To help us walk through the fear.

• • •

Need help walking through the fear? Better ask somebody!

What if we don't have anybody to ask, to grab us and kick us in the seat of the pants? Well, then, as a guy in Los Angeles used to tell me, "You've got to be your own best friend." A best friend is someone who really cares about you. Someone who wants only the best for you. In my opinion, a "best friend" is a person who will tell you the truth about yourself no matter how bad that truth is or how much it might hurt to tell it or to hear it. So, first stand back and take a good *honest* look at yourself. Listen to what you're saying about the situation you're afraid of. But more importantly, pay attention to what you're feeling about that situation. If a little scared is anywhere among those feelings, admit it to yourself. Just say, "Okay, I'm scared." There is nothing unmanly about being afraid. It's perfectly normal to be scared of failure or new situations or things you've never done. Fear sometimes prevents me from coming face to face with people and situations. But mostly, fear keeps me from facing myself. Looking in the mirror used to be hard for me. Sure, I looked at myself to shave, comb my hair, or bust a zit. But really taking a good look at myself, looking deep inside, was hard. Something told me that I might not like what I saw in the mirror when I looked really hard. So, I was afraid to look. It's important to look in the mirror, face your fear and accept it. It's a part of you. Embrace it. Hug it like a big ugly Teddy bear. Then take that fear with you through the fire. Tell someone about your fear. Ask him to walk with you. If you believe in a

God or a Higher Power, admit your fear to him or her and ask them to remove your fear and make your feet move through that fire. But remember a God or Higher Power often works through people. So while your head is bowed and you're praying silently for divine intervention, look up and around you; help may be right in front of your face. Very often the help we need has already been made available to us. But we must reach out to get it. Reach out with your voice and ask another human being to help you through.

President Franklin Roosevelt said once, and I've always liked the sound of this: "The only thing we have to fear is fear itself." Gentlemen, no truer words were ever spoken. If we let it, overwhelming fear will knock us down, keep us down, and defeat us sure as sugar!

the time
i tried dying

Learn first what it is to live.
When you have tried that and don't like it,
then die if you will.
—TERENCE, *The Self-Tormentor*, 161 B.C.

Soon after I started junior high school fear became my closest traveling companion. It seemed seventh grade was the year we were supposed to start growing up. All of a sudden girls and boys were in separate gym classes. We were required to shower after class because we had begun to smell like adults. And everybody was naked in the shower. In the boys' case that led, of course, to visual comparisons of penis size. After my first seventh-grade shower I tried everything I could to avoid showering with the other guys. I was honestly afraid the fellas would laugh at the size of my penis. In fact, through high school I tried to avoid gym class altogether. Or, at least I waited until everyone else showered before I took mine. The reason for this fear was way back in grade school I had heard all black men had large penises. Like lots of other people—adults included—I believed that myth. I actually thought something was wrong with me because I possessed what was, in my opinion, a "wee willie." In addition, adding insult to this supposed injury, I wasn't very good at sports either. Again, I had come to believe the stereotype that all black men were exceptional athletes—so did most of my friends. All of us, like most boys, believed that our athletic ability was a primary measure of our manhood. So there I was in seventh grade: a black boy with what I believed to be a small penis, and even smaller athletic ability. Believe me, it didn't take long for fear to settle in alongside those two major inadequacies. I can only recall guys laughing at my penis a couple of times, but I seem to recall being ridiculed about sports stuff a lot. I was usually the last guy picked in my neighborhood when folks were choosing up sides. It seemed that no matter how hard I ran, I rarely caught that long pass or that high fly ball. When I did hit an occasional lay-up, that absolutely made my day.

I also felt hampered because instead of heading to the basketball court after school, like many of the other guys, I had to head home to practice the piano or the guitar; then I had to do my homework. Friends used to knock on the screen door and ask me to come out. But I knew that there'd be no ball playing till four-thirty when Mom got home and I had finished my practicing. A few of the guys would call me names: punk, sissy—things like that. One of the more regular names I heard was "Uncle Tom." I knew that was a word for a black person who went out of his way to please white people. Back then I could never figure out what that "Uncle Tom" business was all about. Today I understand that some of the kids in the neighborhood called me a "Tom" simply because they saw some of my extracurricular activities as being different from what most black kids did. And after a while I began to think that too, that playing classical music on the piano and memorizing long pieces of prose were different from what most black people did. The truth is, none of us kids knew that black folks all over the world were doing, and had always done, the same things that people everywhere do. Our world extended only to the few square blocks of our neighborhood. We figured if we didn't see black folks doing a particular thing, then black folks just didn't do that particular thing. Because I played classical music and memorized prose I thought there really was something wrong with me. I thought I wasn't really acting black enough to be black, or man enough to be a man. And I was right. There was something very, very wrong with me. That was the very real fact that, as I traveled on my journey, I was letting those guys from my neighborhood walk beside me and whisper in my ear, telling me how I should feel about myself.

I kept playing the piano. Partly because Mom made me, but also because I liked it. At the same time, I didn't get much better at sports. Probably because I didn't practice sports nearly as much as I practiced the piano and the guitar. But on the days when I got called names and I had to fight or run home from school to keep from getting jumped on, I would have traded every note of every song I could play just to catch a football or hit a lay-up—just to be cool in the eyes of the fellas.

Our small, one-bedroom house on Des Moines' east side sat next to a dirt alley. Across the alley from us lived a boy we called the "Commodity Kid." Some of us neighborhood kids had given him that name because of the empty commodity food cans that spilled out of his garbage all the time. When I was a boy there was no such thing as food stamps. Instead, once or maybe twice a month, poor people went down to the county building and got "commodities": basic foodstuffs like flour, peanut butter, peaches, pears, sugar, a long narrow box of truly nasty-tasting cheese, and, of course, Spam. That's what filled this kid's garbage: mostly big, empty, thirty-two-ounce cans of Spam, which is just ground-up pork shoulder and ham packed in a hazy orange-yellow gel that makes a quick slurping sound when it slips from the can. Now, in my neighborhood nobody really wanted to admit that they were poor, so most of us hid our commodity cans way down at the bottom of our garbage. It's not that those of us who received commodities were ashamed, exactly, it was just that hiding the cans kept people from talking about you when they played around your house. Because somebody was always baggin' on somebody else about one thing or another, and how poor somebody was came up a lot. I had seen those commodity cans and that big, fat, bald-headed kid across the alley for years. But around seventh grade fear made me start watching him a lot more closely.

All the neighborhood kids knew that the Commodity Kid was "teched," which was our word for crazy. Sometimes I'd watch him from my mother's bedroom window, which looked out across the alley and into his backyard. The "kid" was about twenty and his folks had this rusted-out Ford Galaxy 500 sitting on four flats in the yard. The car's rear window was busted out. The vinyl seats were cracked. Big wads of stuffing popped out everywhere. There were at least a dozen forty-ounce Pabst Blue Ribbon beer bottles sitting empty in the backseat, but the radio worked. Three or four times a week at about sunset the Commodity Kid would come out of his back door in a pair of shiny, grease-spotted OshKosh bib overalls with one strap dangling—a gray, used-to-be-white T-shirt that hadn't seen bleach since Lassie was a pup, riding up over his belly, his biceps squeezing an open can of commodity Spam and a single row of wrapped saltine crackers directly under his armpit. His left hand stayed in his pocket to hold the side of the bib with the unfastened strap slightly higher than his underwear. Farther down his arm, away from the Spam and crackers, the thumb and index finger of his right hand would almost touch around a forty-ounce bottle. With rations in hand he would go high-stepping through the knee-high grass and weeds that got cut maybe once a season. He would be careful not to drop the Spam as he eased his left hand out of his pocket and opened the door of the Ford a bit so he could catch it with his hip and bump it open wide enough to plop backward into the seat. Although the kid looked slow, he was quick with his feet and would stop the door just as it was about to rebound on his ankle. Next thing you know he'd swing his legs in, turn himself facing the wheel, then set his meat, brew, and crackers beside him on the seat.

Then he'd start to get comfortable: shifting around a little bit, adjusting the seat, just as if he were getting ready to go somewhere. He'd reach over and turn the radio way up loud and the music would come popping and crackin' out of those old rear speakers below the broken rear window. And he'd be gone then, boy. Bobbing his head to the music. Sitting there with his arm across the back of the seat as if he were talking to somebody, laughing and stuff. This was the Commodity Kid's big date, featuring Betty the invisible babe. Nobody knew his real name—it didn't matter to any of us what his name was anyway. He was just a nut who sat in an old car eating commodities and pretending he was on a date.

I laughed at the Commodity Kid when my friends were around. When I was alone, though, I mostly felt sorry for him and sorry for myself at the same time. Because in the back of my mind I was afraid I'd end up just like him: alone, with no friends, talking to an imaginary girl in a rusted-out car in broad daylight. As I watched him across that dirt alley I made a silent vow not to end up like the Commodity Kid.

To keep that vow I studied the Commodity Kid to learn

everything people felt made him laughable and goofy. I committed myself to doing everything possible to be as cool as possible and thus avoid his fate. In the bathroom I would stand before my image in the mirror and practice talking hip and black. I started using curse words because the "hip" kids talked like that, as did the super bad black heroes in a wave of new movies. Occasionally I'd get smart with teachers and other adults in the neighborhood because that's what the other cool kids did. I even laughed at other kids who were being made fun of so maybe the kids would forget to laugh at me. When I went out for football in my sophomore year of high school it was mostly to prove to myself and others that I was really a tough and athletic black kid. But that didn't last long. I played right defensive tackle and the one time I recovered a fumble I ran the wrong way and almost scored a touchdown for the opposing team.

But all through high school I wasn't really sure how I'd keep from becoming the Commodity Kid. I just tried to be cool the best I could. When I got to college, however, I found a tool I felt made me the hippest, slickest, and coolest "dog in the pound."

In college, after I took my first hit of pot, I felt my curse was lifted and I'd never have to be a square, a "Tom," or a sissy ever again. All it took was a few hits and I didn't feel the fear anymore. I could sit down and talk to a girl like a "cool" man was supposed to. And on top of that I could talk in my own style and it didn't sound square anymore. And to my sweet surprise she'd be listening! That old fear that she would laugh me right out of the room was gone. For the first time my own voice sounded good to me—strong, romantic, and hip. I could dance and nobody would laugh. And I wouldn't have cared if somebody did. The music would seep into my bones and move me across the dance floor just the way a hip fella was supposed to. Being good at sports was no longer an issue. And neither was my "wee willie." It was, as I have heard y'all say, "all good."

Drugs made me feel like a man. That joint made me feel good about me. Drugs made it seem as if the world and its people were spinning just the way I wanted them to. As a teenager I'd won trophies for my acting skills, scholarships for my academic achievements, accolades for my musical talents, and the praise and confidence of my mother and a couple of teachers. The praise was nice and helpful and I was proud of my accomplishments, but despite all of that, above anything else I wanted to be "hip, slick, and cool" in the eyes of the fellas. I also believed that if the fellas thought you were cool the ladies would probably think so too. Thanks to the weed and the wine "hip, slick, and cool" were all mine!

Here's the bottom line Gentlemen: the drink and the drugs worked! They made me feel good. They made me *think* I looked good, talked good, and danced good. They made me think that most of what I did was all good. When I was loaded I was carefree and confident. Getting high helped me ignore my fire wall of fear. It also helped me ignore what was really going on with me: the many moments and days when I was not the honorable man I wanted to be. All those moments could be conveniently lost in the feel-good haze of a joint. Being loaded helped me forget (at least for a while) that the world was not always a nice place to live and that I had a responsibility to try to make it better.

There's a guy I like to listen to, his name is Deepak Chopra. Deepak says that "reality is an interpretation." If that is true, then the great danger in my getting loaded was that the drink and the drugs enabled me to "misinterpret" reality any way I wanted—no matter what was really going on with me and the world around me. Loaded, I could easily pretend that what was real *wasn't*. I could even imagine a reality where everything was "cool" and so was I.

When I started smoking weed that first year of college I took these little side trips away from reality and away from myself only every now and then. But by my mid-twenties I was "a frequent flyer." Getting away, feeling good, feeling fearless became an everyday thing. And like I said, it worked for a while—at least it seemed to work. In fact, I might still be soaring today if it weren't for the high cost of flying.

During my two years in the Marine Corps I visited the base chapel every day to practice the piano. In the fall of 1975 while stationed on a small Puerto Rican island called Vieques I discovered a long-sought-after secret: how to combine lyrics and music.

I had started taking piano lessons at age seven. By my fif-
teenth year I had written a couple of songs for my church and
high school gospel choirs. Composing a melody wasn't hard, but
adding lyrics gave me fits. Then, one evening all alone in the
chapel on Vieques, something clicked in my brain and my fingers at the same time. I started hearing the words almost at the
very instant I played the melody and the chords. When I think
back on that time I can still feel the exhilaration of that discov-
ery. It was so good to reach such an important destination on
my journey after traveling so long. Because there had been days
when I almost cried wondering if I would make it there at all.

After that day I wrote songs everywhere. When I left the
Marines and took a day job I'd write on the bus, at work, even in
bed. Writing songs was one way I'd get through a day or night
on many of the make-ends-meet jobs I had. I'd sing and create
new melodies and lyrics while I worked. On the factory assembly line or making burritos at Taco Bell I'd be writing songs in
my head and smiling. After tossing those tacos and doing my bit
on that assembly line I needed to be figuring out how to demo
my songs and get folks to listen. I needed to develop a plan. And
sometimes I would. But sometimes when I wasn't working one
or two of those survival jobs I was smoking a joint and sipping
wine. And, man, that's when the tunes would really start to fly.
But the words and music would fly like the wind and my brain
would be moving in slow motion, so a lot of times I'd miss the
words as they flew by and forget the tune as quickly as it had
come.

The usual picture we get of the guy with a drug or alcohol problem is somebody locked up in jail or living on the street. I've also seen a commercial that shows an egg in a frying pan as a depiction of what a person's brain is like when he's using drugs. That commercial has always seemed a little strange to me. If I were making a commercial about getting high it would go something like this: there'd be a guy sitting in a room surrounded by every conceivable wonderful thing he could ever dream of having. All of these things would be sitting right next to the guy, only one or two feet away. Some of those great things would be only inches away. The guy in my commercial could see all of these things and reach out for them. But no matter how close those fine things were, or how hard he tried to reach for them, he could never actually touch all the stuff he wanted so badly. He could never have them. He could never hold them close and know just how wonderful those wonderful things were.

Sure, I know some guys whose brains were fried by drugs. I know a guy who at fourteen was one of the best tenor saxophone players in the Midwest. At fifteen he was playing with guys twice his age and getting paid. He never lived on the street. Never robbed anybody. Never beat anybody up or caused a scene. I remember a bunch of us gathered in his mom's living room on holidays listening to him play popular R&B songs from the radio. He was truly amazing and I envied his gift. One day after not seeing him for about two years he stopped by a youth center where I was working. I had been home from the Marines for four or five months and it was good to see him. He sat in my little office and we got to talking about all the fun we used to have as kids: the jokes we told; how our parents got on our nerves; all the things we dreamed of doing as kids. Then, all of a sudden, right in the middle of our conversation he stopped talking. I called his name a couple of times but he didn't respond. He just sat there without saying a word, looking off into space. Ten minutes later he started talking again. Right where he had left off. The man didn't miss a beat. At least not in his own mind. It was clear that he was totally unaware he had disappeared right before my eyes for a whole ten minutes. In fact he'd disappeared before his own eyes as well—drugs had taken him away. Today, twenty years later, he still talks about getting another saxophone and playing again. But to my knowledge since that day we talked in my office he never has. Even now in midconversation he vanishes occasionally. In every moment of his life he's surrounded by a world of wonderful opportunities and gifts: music and a master's skill that lives right beneath the tips of his fingers. Audiences of music lovers around the world still wait to hear his genius. Record producers and others in sessions in studios everywhere wait for him to walk in, sit down, and start playing. But the damage drugs have done to his brain prevents him from going out and developing his own skills and having those wonderful gifts and opportunities. I keep thinking that one day he will come back to us. I keep hoping that one day he'll walk through the door of his mom's house with that black and gray case, adjust his reed, and play. How sweet it would be to envy him again.

Gentlemen there's a lot of dry, ugly, vacant ground between an occasional high and that frying pan. It might be better to be like that egg—fried, totally brain dead—than to sit in the center of life surrounded by good things and not be able to get any of them. I didn't drink and do drugs because they made me feel bad. I did them because they made me feel good. Getting loaded made me feel good about me and about life. It even made me feel good about the things I knew I was missing. Loaded, I could dream of the hit record and the starring role in a movie. Loaded, I could reason that I was actually much more talented than those who were "making it," and that the folks who ran the entertainment industry were really afraid of my "large" ability and skills. It would have felt great selling a song or making a record. It would have been a real treat to be a guest on a few television shows. But those kinds of dreams, those kinds of "feel goods" take work and commitment. Achieving those dreams also entails a few "feel bads," disappointments, and setbacks. Getting loaded only took a little money and a lot of time. No "feel bads," no work or real commitment required. Loaded was fast and easy. Following my dreams took time and effort.

Getting loaded seems like the smart thing to do because it appears to make our journeys easier. For me, it made disappointments feel less disappointing. It made me more confident and unafraid. It even made the realization of lifelong dreams seem extremely close and reachable even though in reality, with each high, those dreams were slipping further and further away.

Getting loaded seems a sort of a natural thing because it makes our journeys feel easier. Professional people sip cocktails and wine while talking business. Lots of guys enjoy a brew or two while watching the game. People sip this and that at parties, clubs, and home because it makes laughing, talking, and hitting on "honeys" easier. For billions of people getting a buzz on is as natural as breathing. When something makes you feel good you're inclined to go back to it. If you like playing basketball and slammin' makes you feel good about yourself and your world, you'll probably keep going back to the court. If you like the full, satisfied feeling you get after a burger and fries, you may well find yourself going back again and again for the feeling. Getting loaded is no different. Somewhere between the land of being "Straight" and the land of being "Loaded" there's a border. But it's an invisible border. It's impossible for anyone to say exactly where that border is, but believe me it's there. During that first year of college I started making runs for the border and crossing over into the Land of Loaded. After a few hours I'd head back to the Straight State. It wasn't so bad over there, but loaded felt pretty good, so after a while I'd run for the border again. This time I'd stay a little longer. Over the years my runs became an everyday thing. Sometimes several times a day. Sometimes all day. You see, I never knew that the Land of Loaded and the Straight State were different places. I never even knew there was a border between the two. Then one day when I needed to get back to the Straight so I could get some things done like demo my songs or take a class in how to make it in the music industry, something blocked my way back across the border. Something big, ugly, and broad like one of those evil border guards you see in the old movies. The one who always stops the hero to check his passport and give him a hard time. That day, I made it back to the Straight. But on subsequent trips I started getting delayed regularly by this thing. Oh, I'd get back to the Straight eventually, maybe even get into the studio to do a demo, but after I'd laid the rhythm tracks for my songs I'd run for the border again, forgetting how last time it had been hard for me to get back. And sure enough I'd be delayed. In time I got used to the delay at the border. I just accepted those delays, pulled up a chair, and rolled another joint or poured another glass of wine, and waited. In time I stopped trying to get back altogether. I moved into the Land of Loaded and only made trips back to the Straight to make money to take back with me—'cause if you want to stay in the Loaded you've got to have cash. The Loaded is like the Lotto: no pay, no play. And when you play, you're almost certain to lose.

As I said, just like any other kind of travel my frequent flying was not free. And not only was it not free it was deadly dangerous in a way I never expected. You see when I was away in the Loaded and far removed from myself and reality—the person I was in the Straight—I stopped growing toward manhood. Boys and men are not so different from trees when you think about it. For a tree to grow it has to be firmly rooted in the ground so its roots can feed on the nutrients and drink the water in the earth. A tree needs sunlight in order to stand up straight and tall. The better the nutrients, the more water and sunlight the tree gets, the stronger its roots will be and the stronger the tree. When a heavy wind blows, the tree may bend a little but it won't just fall over. When I was high I was like a sick tree: I wasn't rooted. The soil in the Loaded is hard and rocky. Nutrients for making strong healthy roots are scarce. Although it looked to me as if the sun was always shining over in the Loaded, the only place the sun was shining was inside the world I'd created in my brain. Believe me it's always cloudy in the Loaded. And it's next to impossible for the sunlight of wisdom, reason, and common sense to get through.

In 1978 I rode into Los Angeles in a bright yellow sports car with a pocket full of money. Every day I cruised in the California sunshine: top down, stereo up, and loaded. This went on for months; cruising and playing the player. Many days I promised myself I would go looking for a job. But over in the Loaded, where I found myself daily by about noon, you didn't have to job hunt today because you could always go job hunting tomorrow. In the Loaded the sun was always shining, the money would last forever, and you could always put off paying the car insurance until—you guessed it—tomorrow.

After a couple months of cruising I had a wreck in that yellow convertible; several thousand dollars' worth of damage, no job, and no insurance. Over in the Loaded when the strong winds of life blew my way, when challenged by problems, I failed to find solutions. Instead of bending in that difficult wind and then springing up again with a solution or to do the right thing, I broke. I broke because living in the Loaded had cut me off from the nutrients and sunlight that could have made me stronger, things such as the wisdom and experience of other journeymen and Good Orderly Direction. These are things I had been given in the Straight. Things that would have held me firm and strong. Things I abandoned each time I ran for the border. Over in the Loaded, when the winds of life blew hard I was like a tree whose roots are thin and barely sunk into the ground. Pieces of me snapped in the wind because I had stopped getting the good stuff I needed from the rich fertile soil over in the Straight. I had stopped growing and parts of me were dead, brittle, and weak, so I fell easily in almost any wind that came along. And each time I fell, like a tree fallen in the park, I began to decay.

I never robbed anybody. Never jacked a car, held up a store, or went to jail. Most of the time I worked and sometimes I even excelled at the work I did. I wasn't living on the street or pushing a shopping cart. But I had stopped growing. I had stopped journeying toward my dreams and my destinations. I was stuck, standing still. If our journeys are our lives, then I was actually dying, slowly but surely, decaying little by little. Almost every good thing I did was done so I could stay in the Loaded. I worked lots of overtime during the week so I could cross over to the Loaded on Friday and stay till Sunday night. Then Monday I'd start all over again, making short runs to the border all week long, getting back to the Straight only long enough to get ready for the weekend or to try to fix the damage I had done the

weekend before. I was forever trying to get caught up on the
rent. The car note and other bills. I missed appointments. I
disappointed friends and people I loved over and over again
because I was either stuck in the Loaded or trying to get there.
And the more I stayed in the Loaded the more it became impossible for me to do the hard work necessary to achieve my
dreams, be a friend, or pay my bills. I found that when you get
back after having spent tons of time in the Loaded you find that
much of what you cared about in the world is either falling
apart or gone altogether. I'm talking about family, car, house,
friends, music, and honor. This is the truth about using drugs
and alcohol that never ever occurred to me that freshman year
of college. The bitter truth about drugs and alcohol is that they
were the materials I used to build obstacles in the path of my
own journey. Big obstacles. Roadblocks that eventually stopped
me from suiting up and showing up for life altogether. Whatever fearless feelings drugs and alcohol gave me, I gave pieces of
myself, pieces of my dreams, in return. It was simple: I sold
pieces of my dreams to get high, and then sold more to stay high
so I wouldn't have to face the loss of so many dreams.

Gentlemen, there is lots of ground between a bottle of beer and
a shopping cart. The beer sits in the Straight. The shopping cart
sits in the Loaded. If you can clearly see the border between the
two you'll probably be okay. But if you can't say exactly where
that border is for you, then it's best that you think twice—no,

three, four, or even five times before taking a fix, hit, pill, or drink. I thank G.O.D.—Good Orderly Direction—I got back, but I know a lot of guys who are still out there. Most of them aren't pushing a shopping cart but they said good-bye to the best of their dreams a long time ago.

good orderly direction (g.o.d.)

*What lies behind us and what lies
before us are tiny matters compared to
what lies within us.*

—EMERSON

I wandered around lost in the Loaded for a long time. Most of
the people I knew had no idea that I was lost. Neither did I.

In my mid-twenties I began working for a very popular
radio station in Los Angeles. At that point on my journey it was
the greatest job I had ever had. I wrote radio commercials, created crazy character voices, and even became a weekend D.J.
Man, I was in Hollywood! And all was right with the world! I
thought. I got backstage passes for concerts and hung out at
parties with celebrities. Sometimes I thought about the music I
used to write, or the plays I had acted in, and I'd remember why

I came to Los Angeles in the first place. But by the time I arrived at that radio station, my dreams of becoming an actor and musician were pretty much laid aside. I still wanted those things but I found it easier to go over to the Loaded and fantasize about being a successful artist than to actually do the work required to get it done. It wasn't that I was lazy; I was willing to do what it took to make it in the entertainment industry. It was just that getting loaded demanded so much of me—my time, my money, my energy. Somewhere along the way I began to realize that I couldn't have both: drugs and a career, and I wanted desperately to choose the right path, my career. Unknown to me, however, by the time I understood that I needed to make a choice, I had lost the power to choose.

By the end of my time at the station I had started to miss my dreams. I really missed the music. Sometimes I shied away from going to a movie or to a concert because while 'most everyone else was having fun, I'd be looking at the stage or the screen wishing it was me up there, knowing that I had the talent, skill, and even the experience to be up there. Yet at the same time somewhere inside me I knew that I would never be able to put all those things together to get up there because I was stuck in the Loaded. I couldn't find my way out. I had lost my sense of direction. I had no map to show me how to get back to the Straight. No matter how much I tried I couldn't muster enough power to get onto that stage. The power to accomplish my dreams was sleeping inside me, just as it sleeps inside each one of us, but I had no idea how to find and activate it.

I wasn't always powerless, I reasoned. There were many days in the Loaded when I believed I had power. "Everything's okay," I told myself. I was on the radio every day. I was going to lots of hip parties and hanging out with a few celebrities. Folks would call me up while I was on the air to request a song or to invite me over after I'd finished working. Complete strangers would smile at me and shake my hand when they recognized my voice from the radio. Soon business people from outside the station began asking me to write and produce radio commercials for their companies. I began to make more money and bought a new car. I moved into a bigger apartment. Then I started writing freelance articles for magazines and more money came in. I had power. I wasn't writing music, singing, or acting but I thought, "So what." I was working for the most popular radio station in Los Angeles, hanging out with the stars, and making pretty good money. "Soon," I thought, "I'll get myself a Mercedes and I'll be on top. I'll be a powerful, well-to-do, important guy."

With my "success" I thought I had control over my travels to the Loaded. On certain days I delayed going over to the Loaded or consciously restricted my "flying" until after I had finished my work. But just as often I would get loaded anyway—work or no work. That's when the ideas really flew, I told myself, even though I knew my brain would move too slow to catch them, and when I did manage to hold on to a good idea it might take me twice as long to write that idea down and implement it. So I started compensating for the time I lost taking trips to the Loaded. If I had to produce a commercial by six o'clock and knew I'd probably get loaded sometime that day, I'd start working on the spot several hours before the deadline in order to get it done right. Because in the Loaded I knew I'd make the same silly mistakes over and over again. "Still, no matter," I thought. "I had the power."

When I first started working at the radio station there was this drug called angel dust, or sherman, that was getting a lot of attention. "Sherm heads" were going nuts all over town. According to news reports, angel dust made people insane, and it would take five or six cops to subdue one guy or gal on angel dust. It seemed as though anytime anyone did something really crazy the newscasters would say he or she was on angel dust.

I never used angel dust because I had power. I was hip, professional, and on my way to becoming upper middle class. After a couple of years at the station I had started to produce a series of talk shows. The shows' topics ran from financial management, to sports, to mental health. The people I worked with were doctors, lawyers, and successful business people. They drove expensive cars, lived in rich neighborhoods, and had pretty wives and handsome husbands. A few of these successful folks even took trips to the Loaded now and then. And when they did dope they did only the best dope, only the best weed, only the most expensive alcohol, and only the most expensive drug . . . cocaine. I could see these people had the power. They had cars, houses, and big bank accounts. And they didn't do drugs like angel dust. They didn't drink cheap wine. These people had the power. When they flew, they flew first class! Expensive alcohol. Expensive drugs. I wanted that power too. So I decided never to do angel dust. And I vowed to drink cheap liquor only if I absolutely had to. That's when I began making my trips into the Loaded in a stretch limousine called cocaine. After about nine months in that limo I was more lost than I had ever been. And by the end of that ninth month I had stopped trying to get back to the Straight altogether. As hard as I tried, as much as I wanted to, I just couldn't get back. Nothing could get me back. Not my work. Not the money. Not being on the radio. Not hanging out with celebrities. Not working with successful professional people. Even when my head cleared enough to find the border and I stepped up to the line wanting more than anything to go across, that ugly ol' border guard would step out, throw up his arm, and say "Halt!" And when I looked at his face I'd see the rent I had failed to pay and the eviction notice on my door. In his nasty little grin I'd see the cut-off notice for the light bill and the gas bill. In his cruel laugh I'd realize the days of work I had missed and the people I had let down. I'd raise up on my toes and peek over his shoulder, to catch a glimpse of the Straight and see so many of my dreams sitting neglected and dusty all around me. In the guard's eyes I saw my reflection and the shame on my face. And all those things would taunt me just like an evil, smiling border guard in the movies: "Go on. Go on over to the Straight if you want to," it said.

The border guard would even step out of the way and gesture with his hand to let me pass. But as I stood at that border crying because I wanted to cross so badly, my legs would lock and my stomach would turn and I wouldn't be able to get my feet to move. My body would feel as if it would die if I didn't stay in the Loaded. My heart would beat a mile a minute. My mind would panic at the very thought of having to live in the Straight and deal with all those dusty dreams and all those opportunities I had thrown away. I had come to depend on the haze that always hangs in the Loaded. The haze that seems to make the bad days better and the good days longer. The haze that lets you feel good all the time. The haze that keeps you from seeing things, from seeing yourself as you really are. As I stood there trying to get across, that guard's voice in my head would be saying: "You're going to hurt if you leave. You can't live over there. You've been gone so long, you've messed things up badly. You'll never get it back like it was. You'll never be like you were. Besides, there's lots of pain over there, and if you stay here in the Loaded you won't have to hurt much at all."

"But it hurts now!" I'd say to the guard.

"Nothing's free," he would slither.

"But I might die!" I'd cry.

"Yes," the guard would answer. "But better to die in the haze than to feel the hurt over there."

So on those rare occasions when I was able to find the border, when I got there I lacked the power to cross. So I'd turn around and run deeper into the Loaded believing and hoping that one day I would simply die there and no one would notice. Not even me. Lacking the power to get back on the stage of my dreams, to get back on my journey, I came to believe that my only choice was to die as painlessly as possible.

Long before I got stuck in the Loaded I had been shown lots of maps containing Good Orderly Direction. When I was young, I had seen the maps of religious men and women; youth leaders; teachers; and my mother and Mr. Blue. For sure many folks had given me useful information to help me on my journey. At church I had heard the biblical warning: "Beware of strong drink." In school we watched films that showed the horror of heroin addiction. And, of course, I had seen drunks on the street falling down, talking crazy, and making fools of themselves. But at the same time there were a lot of examples of people using alcohol and drugs with no problem. My mother didn't drink at all, but Mr. Blue always kept liquor in the trunk of his car. So did my uncle and his friends. During family gatherings the men would congregate around the open trunk of the car, sip alcohol, and laugh loud. But not once did I see any of them fall down or make a fool of himself.

When I was growing up, everyone thought that smoking a joint was as harmless as sipping a beer. Even LSD was considered a drug for very smart people. In fact there was a famous doctor who used to drop acid. This college professor suggested publicly that if people really wanted to be aware of what was going on in their world they should drop a few hits of acid. "Turn on, tune in, and drop out," he used to say. Nobody ever *really* talked to me about the dangers of drugs and alcohol. Nobody had to, I thought. I knew that some people drank too much; that drunk drivers sometimes killed people; that junkies stole, slobbered on themselves, and poked holes in their arms with needles. But it never occurred to me in a million years that those things could happen to me. And they didn't! But even though I've never killed anyone, I've never used a needle, or slobbered on myself in a nod, by my late twenties I was as completely lost in the Loaded with no idea how to get back as anyone has ever been. I had been given many maps which warned me about some of the dangers of drink and drugs, but once I was stuck in the Loaded I realized I had no map to show me the way out.

One morning in January of 1983 I caught a glimpse of myself in the bathroom mirror. I was no longer practicing how to talk hip. By that day I had been hip, slick, and cool for years, and it seemed that I had never looked or felt quite so bad. My face was pale, my clothes could have stood up by themselves, and I hadn't had a bath in three days. But there was something else that wasn't right. It was my eyes. They weren't bloodshot, nor had they been blackened in a bar fight. What was wrong was that they weren't looking at me. I couldn't really see myself. My eyes kept shifting away from my own gaze, not wanting to see themselves. When I was able to lock them just long enough for a brief look I saw a stranger in the mirror. "That's not me," I said to myself. "That has to be someone else. I am someone with hopes, dreams, talents, and skills."

I reached for the light to turn it off. All I wanted was to leave the bathroom and crawl deeper into the Loaded. There I could forget what I had seen. There I could resume what I thought was my life. But when I tried to get back I found I was broke, out of paper, no pay no play. I knew in order to stay in the Loaded I would have to go back to the Straight for a short while, to get some more money. But I didn't feel as if I could make it. I had no idea where to get more money. I had borrowed all I could from my friends. I couldn't bring myself to rob anybody, though the thought more than crossed my mind. The only thing I could think to do was call for help. I had thought about asking for help before but not because I thought I was lost. I always thought I could leave the Loaded at any time. I hung tooth and nail to the lie that I had the power. That day in the bathroom I still believed that I had the power. I still believed I could make things right all by myself, but without money to stay loaded I couldn't hold on to that lie. So I called for help.

I spent the next twenty-eight days in a drug treatment center. I was ashamed about the state of my life and all the time I had spent in the Loaded when I first arrived, and expected to be scolded by the people at the center. I expected people to call me weak and stupid. No one did. Instead they smiled, welcomed me, and told me that things would get better. Their smiles and warm words helped ease my fears about returning to the Straight. My neglected and broken dreams still lay on the floor around me, out of reach, but throughout my time at the center no one threw those failures in my face as I expected them to do. Instead they encouraged me to take the maps of my experience in the Loaded out of my bags and look at them. Many of those folks had been just like me. But somewhere, somehow, they had found direction. They'd gotten out of the Loaded and were staying out, as far as I could tell. As I watched them I thought, "Maybe I won't have to die in the Loaded after all." I hadn't come to the center looking for it but soon I realized these people were sharing with me a map of a way out of the Loaded. The longer I was able to stay out of the Loaded—and I've been out for many years now—the more I realized that the map they were showing me had a label at the top: it was called G.O.D., which stood for Good Orderly Direction.

Good Orderly Direction is any information we can gather on our journey that helps us stay out of our own way. As I look back over my journey I am still certain that most of the obstacles I ran into were of my own making. I played a key role in getting to the land of the Loaded. Not once did a bottle jump off the bar, knock me out, and pour itself down my throat. Even the obstacles that other people placed in my path bore the undeniable fingerprints of my own helping hands. Sure I grew up in a time when using drugs was considered a "recreation." There was no "just say no" advertising campaign. When I was a teenager many among the medical community thought weed was not harmful. But even though drugs and alcohol were popular and accepted by my friends, *my* fingerprints were on the bottle and the joint. Others may have passed them to me, but no one forced me to take the hit.

Good Orderly Direction is made up of principles and rules that we use on our journey to prevent ourselves from building obstacles. I get my Good Orderly Direction from all kinds of sources. When I was a kid I got a lot of it from church. Still today I get much of my G.O.D. from Christians, Jews, Muslims, even agnostics. You can find G.O.D. in the Bible, the Koran, and the Torah. I have a Buddhist friend who works with me on "Baywatch" who shares some of the G.O.D. he's gotten from the study and practice of Buddhism. I've found Good Orderly Direction in the presence of homeless people; on airplanes; in the forest; in books; and out of the mouths of people who've never set foot in a church. G.O.D. is simply the things we find that help us on our journey. G.O.D. nourishes us, whether it comes from a line of poetry or a guy sharing his journey. We can get our Good Orderly Direction from almost anywhere. We will know it's G.O.D. if it helps us on our way and if it keeps us out of our own way.

Whenever I'd head off to an audition, my friend Nick would never say "Good luck." Nick always hollered as I went: "Stay out of your own way!" Of course at first I had no idea what he was talking about. But of course I asked and as usual he took the time to share an explanation with me. Often on my way to an audition I would be full of fear and doubt. Will they like my acting? Will I get the role? I'm probably too fat. I bet they're looking for somebody taller. I bet they want someone with more experience. If I get the role, when will they start shooting? And if they start shooting soon, will I get paid in time to pay next month's rent? This kind of thinking would plague me as I drove to the audition, and while I was waiting to go in. It was this kind of thinking, Nick explained, that set obstacles in my path. The energy that I should be channeling toward doing the best audition possible was being channeled into negative thoughts and areas where I had absolutely no influence or control whatsoever. If I was too fat, too tall, or too short, there was nothing I could do about it. There was nothing I could do that day if the producers deemed I was lacking in experience. Both the shooting and the payroll schedule were out of my hands. Would I get the role? That decision was not mine to make. I was blowing my energy worrying about it while I should have been spending that time perfecting my audition. "Do the footwork and leave the results up to G.O.D.," Nick smiled.

In this instance "footwork" meant the audition. The casting decision was up to the producers' G.O.D. For them, Good Orderly Direction meant choosing the actor best suited for the role. If they failed to hire the right actor, the film would suffer. An inappropriate actor would be an obstacle in the path of the film. So you see, everyone has G.O.D. I do the footwork and leave the outcome to G.O.D. And that's exactly what I try to do today whenever I want to reach a destination: I do the footwork—I take the steps—and leave the results up to G.O.D. Maybe no one will choose to read this book. But if I worry about other people's choices, that keeps me from doing the foot-work—which is working on the book today—and the book will never get written. And then the biggest obstacle to this part of my journey will not be the people who chose not to read it, but the man who failed to write it.

Many times an obstacle we place in our path is so huge and overwhelming that for a time the obstacle itself becomes the journey. Just as Ray and Brian had to climb the obstacle of sickness that life had placed in front of them, all too often I must struggle up a steep slope, a mountain of adversity created by my own actions. The time I spent lost in the Loaded was a mountain like that. Once I got stuck over there my journey was simply being lost. If you've ever been lost you know that after a while it's pretty frustrating. And it can get scary too. Can you imagine being lost for years and years and never being able to find your way back to the good places in your life? In a sense that's what it was like for me. Too many of my days were frus-trating, sad, lonely, and scary. Living like that was a struggle. But that's what my journey consisted of, mostly pain and adver-sity. My journey lost in the Loaded was like a daily struggle up a steep rocky mountain. The sad fact is that I built that mountain all by myself. What I've shared with you about my time in the Loaded is the map of my experience on that mountain.

For a long time it was difficult for me to see how my time spent on a self-made obstacle had any value to myself not to mention anyone else. But today it's the map of that terrible experience that keeps me from heading back up that mountain. The more closely I examine my map of that mountain, the time I spent journeying up and down those slopes, the wiser I become about how I got there, what kept me there, and perhaps most importantly how I got off that mountain and back on the right road. Even the mountains of self-made adversity can teach us and make us stronger and wiser if we are willing to examine each demoralizing and difficult step on that bitter journey.

So far on my journey I've received lots of Good Orderly Direction. Much of it, however, I'm inclined to forget. Not only do I tend to forget the lessons that others have shared with me, I often forget to study the map of my own experience—important firsthand experience that might help me stay out of my own way. It is exactly because I tend to forget so many of the details of my journey that it becomes imperative that I share my experience, my map, with others. When I share honestly the map of my journey with you—the good traveling days and the bad—I am compelled to recall the truth about the exact nature of those good and bad days. When I share my map with you I can't help but see the truth about my own journey. It is the honest sharing then that reminds me of where I've been—the wrong turns I've made and the Good Orderly Direction that keeps me out of my way. This may sound strange, but to hold on to the G.O.D., I've discovered on my journey I must be willing to *give it away*. Today this same principle applies to practically all aspects of my life. To hold on to my skill as a pilot I must stay willing to share the joy of flying with others so that they can appreciate the world from a new perspective. In order to keep my acting skills sharp I sometimes use those skills to communicate to others the importance of G.O.D. in our lives. And for sure I try to stay willing to share the map of my journey to and from the Loaded so that others can find their way back to the Straight—and so I will never forget the loss of my own dreams and how difficult it was to uncover them again. For anything valuable in life I believe that to keep it you have to give it away.

If you've ever seen water sitting in a pothole after a rain, you know that even though the water comes from high above, in a few short hours that water will start to look and smell pretty bad. Dirt, bugs, and unseen organisms will take full control of the water in that pothole and make it totally undrinkable. In time that water will dry up altogether. Like rainwater in the pothole, the water in a mountain pool also comes from a higher place: snow that has melted farther up the mountain. But new water flows into the mountain pool as the water already in the pool flows out and on down the mountain. Unlike the water in the pothole, the water in the mountain pool stays full and fresh because new water is always flowing in and the old water in the pool is always flowing on. Hopefully our journeys are like the mountain pool. The Good Orderly Direction we receive is like new water flowing into the pool from a higher place. The Good

Orderly Direction we give to others is the water in the pool that flows on down the mountain filling and refreshing other pools and then moving on. It's the flow of the G.O.D., the giving and the getting, that keeps our pool of Good Orderly Direction full, fresh, and usable.

grace

God made the sea, we make the ship;
He made the wind, we make a sail;
He made the calm, we make oars.
—SENEGAL PROVERB

While I was in the center, I was given access to the maps of other folks' experience, folks some of whom had been lost in the Loaded a lot longer than I had. Folks who had found maps that showed them the way out.

One day, at the center, I asked these people where they'd found the power to draw such good and wonderful maps. They looked at me like I was kind of crazy and said they didn't draw these maps, and they didn't have any power. They got their direction from something called "grace." I looked up the meaning of grace and one definition was "unearned blessing." What they meant was that it was not by their own power that they had managed to get out of the Loaded. This was a familiar idea because I had tried for a long time to get out but couldn't find the way myself. These people told me that grace was like a pair of guiding hands that turned them when they were lost and gave them a gentle push in the right direction.

Grace was a divine compass that pointed the way out of the Loaded. Very often that grace is carried to lost people by other people—people giving away what they've learned in order to keep it. This carrying of grace to lost people had been going on well before I was even born. I used to wonder who was the first person to carry this grace to a lost boy or man? And where did that first person get the grace to carry? Where does grace come from? I asked myself. All I could come up with is that that first compass, that first package of power, that first bit of grace that gave direction to that very first lost person must have come from something much bigger, much more powerful than that person, or any person for that matter. Slowly I came to believe that grace is the gift of a higher power. It is a very big and important gift, often carried to lost people by other people.

The wonderful thing about grace is that it is carried to us whether we want it or not. When I first entered the rehab center it was only because I was scared of facing the facts of my life. But in my first few hours in the center people I didn't even know started bringing me the grace of that higher power. One way they did that was by simply listening to me and understanding me. I had expected to be scolded for being stuck in the

Loaded. I had expected people to call me weak and stupid. No one did. The people at the center smiled, welcomed me, and said that things would get better. Their smiles and warm words helped ease my fears about returning to the Straight. And when I talked to them about my fears and despair no one said I was washed up. Instead they nodded and then told me a little something about themselves. The kindness and compassion that these people carried to me were like guiding hands that set me in the right direction. And they did it without my asking.

Grace, then, is a pair of hands and a compass that head us in the right direction. And grace is often carried to us by others. Grace is brought to us when we call for help. Even if we call for help for the wrong reasons. No matter when or where we find ourselves lost on our journey, help is available to us through the power of grace. All that seems to be required for us to have grace delivered is a call for help.

Once I asked for help, by grace folks came and showed me some good direction. I was still lost in those early days at the center, and I spent many lost days after leaving. But it was by grace—delivered by others—that I received my first glimpse of the maps that could eventually lead me back to the Straight. Now, I didn't say that those maps of others' experiences "would" lead me back. I said they "could." You see, after I had received grace it was time for me to do some legwork. Grace, a pair of guiding hands, only turns us in the right direction and maybe gives us a slight push down that road. But to move forward with Good Orderly Direction we have to suit up and show up, and put one foot in front of the other. The counselors, doctors, and people at the center freely shared their maps with me. However, in order to use those maps to get out and stay out of the Loaded, I had to listen. I had to study those maps. I had to put them in my bag and be willing and able to pull them back out when I thought I needed them. Often at the center I listened but failed to pay close attention. I didn't study those maps and rarely did I put them in my bag for the journey, although it was clear to me that these folks had been as lost as I had. I knew that the maps they'd gathered had led them back to the Straight. Certainly their descriptions of time spent wandering in the Loaded and their futile attempts to get back to the Straight were almost identical to mine. There was no doubt these folks had received the gift of grace. After years of being sad, lost, and without honor they were now not only achieving their dreams but were dreaming and fulfilling new ones! People who had always dreamed of going to college, owning businesses, or just being helpful to others were doing all of those things. So I *knew* in my head that I should be listening hard to these folks and taking whatever I could from their journeys to help me stay out of the Loaded, but I would fail to study their maps and would find myself back across the border, face to face with that stranger in the mirror.

And so I called for help again. And again. And again. And each time I would find grace, or rather it would find me, and I'd journey back to those people and listen again to their stories. And each time I'd try harder to listen to what they were saying, hoping that one day I could hold the maps of Good Orderly Direction in my hand, in my heart, and in my bag for my journey. No matter where we find ourselves on our journey, grace is like a compass, a compass that always points us back toward Good Orderly Direction; and it is always available to us. All we have to do is ask for it.

Because each of us has to make our journey alone we usually get lost alone. We can wander for days, months, even years, alone. Some people can see that we are lost. When they tell us what they see we get angry and deny that we are lost at all.

When being lost gets scary enough we usually call for help, if only to find a safe place to be until the fear goes away. The trick is staying alive long enough to get scared enough to call for help. Sometimes being lost can be very dangerous. The Loaded is a place where a man can die long before he gets scared enough to call for help. And a man can get lost in other dangerous places too. I've known some guys who were lost in violence. Boys and men who died or were crippled before they were able to call for help. There are even some guys who got lost trying to make money. These fellas got so caught up trying to get paid that they neglected other important things in their lives like family, friends, and honor. They wandered around in the finest clothes, the biggest cars, with pockets full of cash, willing to do anything to get paid. Sometimes these guys ended up in jail. That's how deeply they were lost in the money. I'm not just talking about dope dealers and such. I'm talking about lawyers, stockbrokers, doctors, businessmen, and the presidents of big banks. Men who were already millionaires. Men who were so lost in the money that not even millions could make them who they wanted to be. Many of those guys—the ones lost in money and violence—are better now because of grace. Some were lost in the money. Some were lost in the violence. I was lost in the Loaded. But lost is lost. And grace was there for all of us when we called for help.

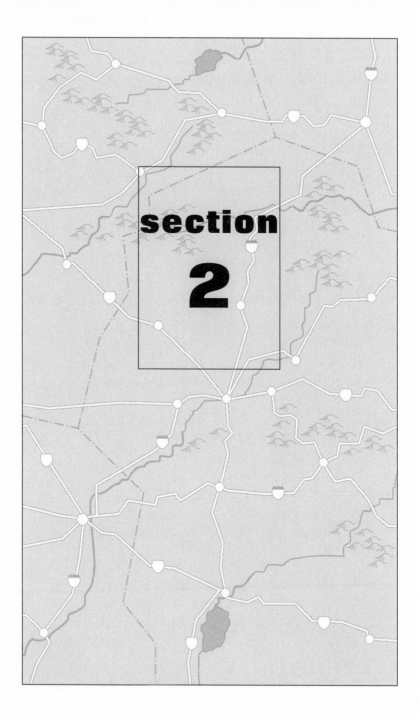

section

2

a single garment
of destiny

All for one, one for all.
—ALEXANDER DUMAS, *The Three Musketeers*

I'm a professional forgetter. I need to be reminded about a lot of things. Thank goodness when I pull up to a busy intersection there's a big red sign or very visible light reminding me that other drivers and pedestrians are using the road. Each day that I suit up and show up for another session of life, other people show up too. There's you and me and lots of folks on the "life" road. But often I forget about you and those other traveling folks and I need to be reminded to stop, slow down, and look out for others. When I look out for others I'm also looking out for myself because if I run a stop sign or go through a red light not only do I risk hurting others I also risk hurting myself. Dr. Martin Luther King Jr. said, "we are tied in a single garment of destiny." That means that very often the things we do as individuals affect not only ourselves but others. And buzzing through stop signs and stoplights can affect a lot of other folks, folks we don't even know.

Sometimes on my journey I hurt other people with the things I say and do. I know it's not right. I know that my words and actions can hurt people, but I forget sometimes and I don't stop. There are times too when I don't want to stop. And since there's no sign telling me to slow down and watch out for the other guy's feelings, I just keep going—ZOOM!—right through. I might be in a bad mood. I might not like someone because at some point I remember them running right over my feelings. It might be that I don't like where a person comes from, or where she goes to church, or his ethnicity, her gender, or who he sleeps with. Whatever it is, it's all about my being intolerant of another human being. And that intolerant state of mind tells me it's okay to call names and try to make folks ashamed of who they are. It might even tell me to threaten them physically or to steal their liberty by abusing them physically. These are the times when I need you guys to remind me what it's like to be made to feel ashamed. Or how it hurts to be physically and verbally abused. I need you guys to remind me to slow down, to stop and consider the other guy's feelings and the other guy's property—the other guy's liberty. Many times on our journey we may do the wrong thing because we think no one is looking or that no one really cares. A couple of years ago I saw a riot on the television news. A pleasant-looking, nicely dressed lady was pushing a cart along a grocery store aisle picking out her favorite brands. Meanwhile, all around her folks were running back and forth with armloads of stuff, looting the store. Of course the shopping lady was looting too, though she was taking her time and looting quite calmly. The next thing you know, up stepped a news reporter who asked, "Miss, why are you stealing this merchandise?" The lady thought for a moment, then replied with a grin, "Nobody's stopping me."

There will be times when I need you guys to stop and remind me that what I am doing to others and to myself is wrong. I will need you guys to be stop signs and stoplights for me. But don't hit me over the head. Because all that'll do is make me mad and shut down my ears. Just remind me.

There will be days too when I will need you to be my "spark." There will be times when just slowing down and stopping will not be enough. There will be times when I need to get out of my car and actually get into action. And that's when I may need you to be my spark and light a fire under my rear end in order to get me moving in the right direction. Just like a spark plug for an engine: without that spark, internal combustion cannot begin and the engine will not run. If my courage, like that engine, is cold, I may need your sense of justice to remind me of what is right and your courage to spark my courage so that I can get into action.

You've seen those movies where the officer stands up on the battlefield in front of his men, waves his sword, and leads the gallant soldiers into battle. Well that's exactly what I'm talking about here. Except I'm not suggesting you travel to another country, or another neighborhood, or another street to kill anyone. I'm suggesting that you and I should stand up in our own home, school, town, church, and neighborhood and wave others forward in support of liberty and justice for all. After all as Americans we've all taken a pledge of allegiance and part of that pledge is a promise to preserve liberty and justice for *all*.

Liberty can be defined as the right to make our journey without being made to feel ashamed or afraid as we go. Often part of looking out for others is just standing up, raising our voices and our hands in order to draw attention to the theft of another person's liberty.

Consider this: a man gets his wallet stolen. He starts jumping frantically up and down crying, "Stop, thief . . . Stop, thief, somebody stole my wallet!" Only one other person hears him. That one person stops what he's doing, turns around, and sees the thief. He gets excited, starts jumping up and down as if he's on fire. He calls other people's attention to the theft, and he says to a person nearby, "Hey, did you see that? That guy just stole a wallet." Then the second person waves down a passing police car. Then another person down the street hears the news that a wallet was stolen, and she makes a mental note of a man running down the street with a wallet in his hand. Then a couple of other folks begin chasing the thief down the street. When the fleeing thief looks back over his shoulder he sees not only his victim screaming his head off, he also sees other people screaming their heads off, watching him, summoning the police, and even a couple of folks chasing after him. Instantly the thief realizes he didn't rob one guy. He robbed five or six! Who knows, maybe the thief will drop the wallet or think twice next time about robbing someone. Perhaps as he climbs the mountain of consequences he has set in his own path he will grow wiser and more aware of the role he has played in making his journey more difficult. If he is willing to study this map of his own experience, he may never have to climb the same obstacle again.

So in this case the victim lit a spark. He called for help. That call for help was a spark that started a chain reaction. The people who heard his call and who felt that spark were like the cylinders of an engine as they began moving to his aid.

There have been many times in human history when groups of people just stood around and watched while one person or a few people were robbed of their liberty. What might have happened if just one person had raised his voice on behalf of those being robbed? Might others have joined them in calling for an end to the theft?

Most of us want to do the right thing. Part of the problem is that often we are afraid to be the first to step forward and speak up for what's right. So, fellas, when liberty is being stolen one of us must be the first to step forward and raise our voice on behalf of what is right. There are days when I will need you to spark a fire within me so that I will watch out for others and get into action on their behalf. Of course there is no guarantee that when you act as a spark, when you stand up and wave that sword, that others will catch fire and follow. There is no guarantee that you'll be surrounded by lots of other folks looking to do the right thing. But there have been all kinds of people who served as sparks for others without a guarantee that they would be successful. Lots of folks followed George Washington across the Delaware as he pursued freedom. Lots of folks followed Cesar Chavez when he lit a fire for justice under the feet of migrant workers. Lots of folks followed a woman named Ida B. Wells when she lit a fire under them to settle the Oklahoma territory at the turn of the century. There was no guarantee that others would heed these calls, but George, Cesar, and Ida B. made themselves that "spark" anyhow. And it may have taken a little time but others did come. The odds are in your favor that others will follow when you light a fire under them, because it's very doubtful that in any situation where liberty is being stolen, you will be the only person who realizes that a theft is taking place. Go on, gentlemen, be a stop sign for justice, be a spark for liberty. You won't be the only person who wants to do the right thing. You just may be the only one willing to step forward first.

the forty
kinsmen

---

the magnificent power of the ''we''

We must all hang together,
or assuredly we shall all hang separately.
—BENJAMIN FRANKLIN

Once upon a time forty Kinsmen were brought before the King and accused of excessive industriousness and ingenuity. All of the Kinsmen were masters of a craft, and each worked unceasingly from sunrise to sundown, pausing only for the shortest amount of rest. Among the Kinsmen there were carpenters, teachers, tillers of the field, falconers, masons, mathematicians, cooks, caretakers of the vine and limb—masters of every conceivable art and skill. The Kinsmen took pride in their individual knowledge and accomplishments. But, unknown to the Kinsmen, their knowledge, success, and industriousness had greatly disturbed the King. You see, the King and his ministers feared that the Kinsmen were becoming too rich and too powerful and enjoying far too much of the people's respect. And when the King and his ministers considered the collective wealth, power, and respect which resided among the forty Kinsmen, the enormity of the perceived danger caused the King himself to shudder with fear. Clearly, the King and his ministers agreed, something had to be done. And so the forty Kinsmen were rounded up and arrested.

"Master Kinsmen," said the King's first minister in a loud and pretentious voice, "you all stand accused of pilfering the love and admiration of the people. A level of love and admiration which has forever been, and should, therefore, forever remain the pure and indisputable province of the King. Master Kinsmen, how do you plead?"

For the next several hours, one by one, each of the forty Kinsmen stepped forward to plead his or her innocence. For not one among them had deliberately sought to usurp the King's due. Their only desire had been to perfect their skill and to labor humbly till the end of their days.

After each Kinsman had spoken his and her piece, the King and his ministers retired to an inner chamber to consider the verdict. As the deliberations developed behind closely guarded doors the forty Master Kinsmen themselves retired to forty separate parts of the vast gathering hall to await word of their fate. The wait, as you might suspect, was brief.

"Master Kinsmen," began the minister, "you have been found guilty of the theft of the King's property—namely, the honor and respect of the King's subjects. As of this day you are no longer considered forty Master Kinsmen but rather forty Thieves who will, with the next rising of the sun, find full use of the executioner's ax."

Although the forty Kinsmen received the verdict in forty separate corners of the courtroom they were now collectively silent, collectively shocked, and collectively condemned. Not one of the eighty ears among them could believe they had been so falsely accused, not to mention so cruelly condemned.

Then, quite coolly, the minister continued: "The King being of a benevolent spirit has allowed for the possibility of a reprieve."

At this the eighty ears of the forty Kinsmen pricked up instantly.

"In the King's courtyard lies a stone," announced the minister. "If, before the sun shows itself tomorrow, any of those now condemned can move that stone he or she shall be granted amnesty and find himself or herself restored to the property and position previously possessed."

Without delay the forty Kinsmen rushed from the court chamber, down the stone stairways, and out into the King's courtyard. No sooner had they entered the courtyard than they stopped, frozen in forty separate places by the sight of a single huge white stone which rose like a temple high above them. Rectangular in shape, mammoth in height and girth, the forty Master Kinsmen gazed not only upon the stone itself but upon the hopelessness of their fate as well. At that moment and in that hopelessness forty condemned Thieves fell to their knees and began to pray forty fervent prayers. Each sincere but separate prayer beseeched God to grant the executioner a sharp and painless ax.

Some hours passed as the forty Kinsmen continued to pray for the divine hand of God. And their simultaneous but very separate requests for divine intervention did indeed reach heaven but only as the whisper of forty autumn leaves somersaulting in a gentle wind.

Suddenly, one of the forty rose to her feet, her face flushed with crimson determination. In the next instant she was running, leaping, racing forward toward the stone. A warrior's scream tore from her lips as her entire body fell upon the thick and solid mass of the stone. Flesh and sinew stretched and strained against the weight. The force of her effort dug trenches in the earth. Sweat seeped from her back and brow. Her fingers leaked purple blood as she clawed at the immovable stone. Finally, trembling and spent, she hung her head and fell to her knees. But as she fell another Kinsman rose and ran toward the stone with lowered shoulder and high hopes, for these forty Kinsmen so falsely accused were laborers, not afraid of hardship and toil. And it was in that spirit, in that tradition, that one by one they rose and threw themselves against that rock. And those among them who were masters at cutting stone made haste with their tools to whittle away a pound of stone, or two or five or ten.

Then others rushed the stone and swore; broke their bones and cried. The engineers among the Kinsmen privately searched their knowledge and experience for a means of moving the stone. And as those engineers studied the situation individually, one very bruised, broken, and condemned Kinsman squinted toward the east and spied the first yellow-orange locks of the sun as it woke from its sleep behind the mountains. This sight brought the certainty of death crashing down on the already sorrowful heart of this Kinsman. And with the sourness of that sorrow rising from his belly and curdling in his throat, a scream burst from him and fell upon the ears of his fellows.

"My God, my God, we are condemned to die!"

At that moment each of the forty Kinsmen turned his head toward the mountains where the sun was now on its feet and beginning its walk across the sky. Forty separate cries of sorrow rose with the sun. And as sun and sorrow rose so did the one bruised and battered Kinsman who had first seen the sun and awakened them all to their fate. That one Kinsman now began limping toward the stone, shuffling sideways, one cracked and twisted hand dangling uselessly at his side. In an instant this Kinsman was joined by others with bent backs and broken shoulders, dragging fractured feet and legs. First ten, then twenty-five, soon thirty, then all forty moved and moaned toward the stone: in hopelessness and desperation they went. Many prayed as they lurched forward that this final, futile assault would finish off their bodies and spare them the humiliation of the headsman's ax. On and on they came until at last *all forty fell heavily and simultaneously upon the stone!* . . . and the stone . . . moved.

The King and his minister, who had also risen with the sun, were looking out on the courtyard as the stone moved. The King shrugged his shoulders and went back to bed. The King's minister apologized to the executioner and assured him that he and his ax would have their day. The minister then told the soldiers to disperse the disappointed crowd that had gathered for the execution. Finally the King's minister dismissed the forty Kinsmen after officially informing them of their reprieve and restoration to their former property and rank.

For a thousand years the story of the forty Kinsmen was passed from father to daughter. From mother to son. From government to government. From campfire to campfire. And as new stones arose new Kinsmen practiced the lesson that had been learned in the King's courtyard. When confronted by a seemingly immovable obstacle, for example stones of tyranny, intolerance, and hard times, these Kinsmen, like their forebears, gathered deliberately and without delay and threw themselves against the stone. In fact the story of the King's stone became the very foundation of the Kinsmen's society. No longer was each Master Kinsmen a master of his or her fate alone. No longer was hardship met individually, separately, and privately.

Now a fate that confronted one confronted all. For it was only when the Master Kinsmen united and threw themselves upon the stone together did each individual Kinsman escape the executioner's ax.

In all things, the Kinsmen recalled the stone and the truth it had shown them—that when one Kinsman was besieged they were all besieged. That when one Kinsman's limbs lay in the path of hardship's stone, all Kinsmen must rise with her and lay their shoulders to the task of preserving liberty and justice for the one, so that there might be liberty and justice for all. And this commitment to preserve liberty and justice for all was made part of the repeated pledge the Kinsmen took when they remembered and honored the forty who had first fallen upon the stone. Man, woman, and child swore this oath facing their flag, hats and hearts solemnly and sincerely in hand.

A few years ago a city of the Kinsmen burst into flames as mobs swept through the streets. Again the stone raised itself high, dwarfing the helicopters that swarmed around it. The stone of intolerance, violence, and despair rose at an intersection while descendants of the first forty stood silently in its shadow and watched others of their number beat the innocent and burn their dreams. It was clear that many of the Kinsmen, both the bystanders and the batterers, had forgotten the lesson and the wisdom of the stone. But there were those there that day who remembered the story. There were many who drove wounded

Kinsmen to hospitals and hid them in their homes. As they dragged their fellow Kinsmen to safety they also dragged the discarded story of that first stone across the courtyard of the attackers' conscience. A few of the attackers remembered the stone and put down their hatred. There were others there who remembered the stone and turned to help their brother put down the weapon he held above his head.

The story these Kinsmen had learned may have been set in a different time and place from the story of the first forty Kinsmen. In the story they knew it may not have even been a stone that was moved by the many, nor forty Kinsmen who moved it. Perhaps the story they'd heard was not a tale told by a grandmother at fireside, or a grandfather at bedside. For you see, over time, the lesson of the stone can be found anywhere and everywhere, among any people: in their holy books and books of virtue; in the lyrics of their poets; in the pledges of their patriots, and in the farmer's field and the scholar's study. For the story of the stone is wisdom that falls naturally upon every person who yearns for freedom and justice. And so, there were many that day in the Kinsmen's city who knew, in their own way, of the stone. Many who stood steadfast in the face of the brutal, hateful rock that shadowed an intersection in the burning city.

Within the intersection there was a Ford Bronco, and at the rear of that Ford Bronco was a dark old Kinsman standing with his arms outstretched holding off the attackers with his body. There was another Kinsman there too, a university student soon to become master practitioner of the Law. This student stepped from his vehicle to help a fallen Kinsman and in so doing threw himself against the stone of bigotry, violence, and the stone of death itself. Then there was a Kinsman long in years with tears in her eyes who leapt upon that stone by calling from her front porch: "Do you want me to call 911?"

And there were ten more who stood observing the madness a block or two away from the intersection. One among them pushed hard against the stone when he laid a bloodied Kinsman on his lawn. A Kinsman, middle-aged, laid both hands solidly and defiantly against the stone's surface when she emerged from her home with a towel to wipe the bloodied Kinsman's wounds. The eight others still on the corner lay their backs on the stone when they summoned a passing police cruiser. Within moments, another who knew the story of the stone came around the corner in a small car full of children: "Can I take him to the hospital for you?" the young Kinsman asked. With these words and willingness she dug her heels into the ground and in a single compassionate stroke brilliantly brought the stone's saving wisdom to each and every one of the small spongelike minds seated around her. And I do believe it was at that moment that they all felt the ugly, indifferent, and intolerant monolith move, just a bit. And finally there was one more, one more beautiful dark Kinsman in a Chevy van, a rough-looking fellow with a scarf on his head. It was that van and the courage of this Kinsman that carried the fallen Kinsman to the hospital and provided the final ounce of strength needed to move the stone clearly and unmistakably. All across the city, as battered Kinsmen made their way to the safety of surgical rooms and hospital beds, an entire nation of Kinsmen saw the stone move.

These days those who recall the story of the stone are called Heroes and Sheroes. Perhaps you have heard the wisdom of the stone. Maybe you have not carried a sword or pulled a Kinsman from a mob. Maybe you have yet to feed a hungry person. But when you preserve justice on behalf of another's journey, you are a man who has left his mark upon the stone. Continue to live the lesson of the stone. Teach all and remind those who have forgotten that they too are their brother's keeper: that you and they and all of us are tied in a single garment of destiny. Perhaps in time there will be no need for heroes such as yourselves. No heroes, only Kinsmen who recall the wisdom of the stone.

violence

---

*To call war the soil of courage and virtue
is like calling debauchery the soil of love.*

—GEORGE SANTAYANA

You and I have been groomed for war almost from the time of
our birth. As children, little girls were given dolls to nurture and
cuddle. You and I were given guns to play make-believe murder
in the guise of a deadly game called war. Perhaps we were allowed to play war games so that when our community called us
away from our everyday lives to kill other little boys we would
go willingly, thinking that we were going out to play. The popular notion is that males go to war as boys but return as men. And
I always believed that war made men out of boys. I have, however, begun to wonder: is there nothing else that can make a

man? Is there no manhood, no strength, in peace, compassion, and charity?

On the battlefield a boy's death is called the "supreme sacrifice." In other words the height of sacrifice is how a boy dies and not how he lives. Does this mean sacrifice and service spread over a lifetime are of less value than dying in the midst of violent conflict?

In wartime the deaths of civilian women and children are a frequent occurrence. These tragic occurrences are rightly called "atrocities." When boys and men and women fall in battle, however, their deaths are called "casualties"—*casual*-ties. Those of us who have lost friends, brothers, sisters, fathers, mothers, cousins, uncles, aunts, sons and daughters to violent conflict know that there is absolutely nothing *casual* or easy about their deaths.

I wonder today why I so readily accept the violent death of a man while I am so appalled at the violent death of women and children. The news report of a woman's or child's murder makes me sad and angry. A similar report of a man's death rarely affects me as deeply. Perhaps this is because I have been taught that boys and men are by nature more easily subject to violent death, that our position in society is primarily that of warrior. Warrior in the workplace, warrior on the athletic field, in the halls of Congress, beyond the sea, and in "the hood."

Maybe today before I volunteer to kill another man or boy at home or abroad I should stop and think about why I am willing to do so. Does he deserve to die? Is it because he is male that I believe it is his destiny to die violently? Does his journey threaten my journey or the journeys of those I love? And if I see any of these things as true, who taught me this truth? Who told me that this man was my enemy? Has he offended me or did someone *teach* me that his thoughts, his words, or his life offended me? Was it my government or my gang that told me this? Was it the television? My acquaintances?

Or is it that I have embraced the lie that boys are destined to kill boys because that is one of the acts that makes us men?

people
and opinions

To hold our own, we have no time
to spend fretting over nonessentials.
—BOOKER T. WASHINGTON

What other people think of me is none of my business. What I think of myself is most often the yardstick I need to use when trying to measure what kind of man I am. Of course, in order to rely on my own measurement, I must first have a standard of what being a man is. When it comes to developing a standard for manhood I can look at the maps other folks have given me of their journeys. I'll also tell you this: during the course of my journey I've learned to pay more attention to what kind of man a fellow is, rather than what kind of man he tells me I should be.

A couple of years ago it was time for me to buy a new car. I looked at several different models; some I could easily afford, others would have been harder on my wallet. Around this same time I flew to Northern California to share some thoughts with a group of teachers who were exploring new ways of teaching history. A friend's parents picked me up at the airport in a late-model Cadillac. The car looked nice and the ride was cool and comfortable. "Maybe I'll buy a Cadillac," I thought. In the next instant I dismissed the thought as being totally unrealistic. Why?

When I was growing up a lot of the hardworking, success-ful black men in my neighborhood, and indeed all across the country, drove big beautiful cars, including lots of Cadillacs. Success in any community is often defined by a person's ability to purchase big, expensive stuff: houses, jewelry, cars, and the like. For a long time in America, racist laws and attitudes limited black folks in the ways they could assert their wealth. For exam-ple, in communities all over America black men and women were prohibited from buying homes in certain areas of town. Black folks were often banned from expensive stores and restau-rants where they might have spent their many hard-earned dol-lars. Black people could, however, purchase any kind of car they could afford, so naturally, those who could afford the best, bought the best. And Cadillac cars were among the most expen-sive and well-made cars in America. Consequently, today, to many people, a Cadillac has become a stereotype and a shame-ful symbol of black manhood. For many years "brothers" driv-ing Cadillacs have been the subject of jokes and ridicule by people, both black and white. Unfortunately, some people now believe that owning a Cadillac is a sign of a lack of sophistication. And for many years the film and television industry placed only negative and unflattering black characters in the driver's seat of a Cadillac. Today, many of my peers in the entertainment industry, black and white, drive foreign luxury cars. And for sure, the image of the actor, pop star, and sports celebrity in a foreign-made luxury car is accepted by most folks as a sure symbol of success.

That day, as I rode along those Northern California roads in the front seat of a smooth, comfortable car I thought, "A Cadillac car might suit me just fine. I could get a used one and pay cash and not have a car note!" But then I thought, "Yeah, but you know how folks are, they'll probably think I ain't hip. After all, I am on TV. People expect to see me driving a Mercedes or something." I know all this sounds silly. But these are the thoughts that went through my head before I went out and bought a mint-condition 1988 Cadillac with a bumper-to-bumper warranty.

Now let's go back over my so-called reasoning and see what was really going on:

Here are the facts: I am able to eat at least three meals a day. I have a nice place to live. I get to fly airplanes, write books, travel to some pretty interesting places, and spend a lot of time on the beach. Do I really have to drive an expensive foreign car because that's what strangers who see me on TV expect me to drive? Do I really have to drive a certain kind of car so that people will think I'm successful and hip? And who are these people who said that driving a Cadillac was unsophisticated?

Are they going to pay my car note and my insurance, or buy my gas? Why was I letting their opinions roll around in my head? What's really funny is that no one was ever actually going to come up to me and say, "Greg, you really shouldn't buy a Cadillac. If you do, everybody will think you ain't 'all that.' "

So the truth is, what was leading me away from buying a Cadillac were the voices in my head! Other people's voices living in my head *rent-free!* I can't tell you whose voices they were. I mean, I can't really put a face to any of the voices. They were just voices. But the voices were there, right inside my head, making me doubt what was right for me.

And there it is, that fear thing again—the fear of what others might think of me that almost caused me not to do what was best for me.

I wrestled with that Cadillac decision for several months. But one of the things that helped me work through it was sharing my thoughts about buying a Cadillac with those teachers in Northern California. During our conversation I told them about my fears of being perceived as unsophisticated and unhip. I didn't share my feelings with them because I thought they could tell me what kind of car to buy, I shared my thoughts and my fears with them because my journey has taught me that sometimes secrets make you sick. You don't know what to do about something so you keep rolling it around and around in your head until it starts spinning, as if you're on a ride at Disneyland. Instead of getting clearer, the issue gets fuzzier and fuzzier until it makes you sick inside. I was ashamed of these other people's thoughts rolling around inside my head, and I was even more embarrassed that it was so difficult for me to evict those voices. But by just letting it out, and letting others know what I was thinking, I got myself past the shame and embarrassment. And most important, I got rid of the voices. I evicted those voices by sharing them with others. Sure I was embarrassed for having listened, but my embarrassment disappeared almost as soon as I started talking about what was in my head. Some folks smiled, other folks laughed, but that was okay because by sharing I was evicting those secret voices. And after a while, those teachers started sharing with me some of the voices that moved into their heads every now and then. And then I realized that I was not the only person in the room who occasionally allowed the opinions of others to live in his head rent-free.

failure

If you see somebody winning all the time,
he isn't gambling, he's cheating.

—MALCOLM X

Remember, fellas, our failures can work for us if we listen to the lessons that failure has to teach. Failure will always be a very real part of our lives. Past failures are part of our map as future ones will be part of our destiny. All too often we may think of history as boring and unmeaningful. After all, what's yesterday got to do with what's happening right now? Sometimes the experiences that lie behind us, the mistakes that we've made, appear too ugly to look at. They bring back a lot of anger and shame and other stuff we'd rather not spend time looking on. But what's real for me is this: if I don't look back at my map, I mean hold it in my hand and look closely at it, then much of what I've experienced in my life has simply gone to waste. Even if I've taken some wrong turns and built some bad obstacles, my earlier journey can be of great value as long as I examine my map and use it to help guide me on my journey today. Even the fatal mistakes of others can be of great value if I look at those mistakes closely.

I used to be a smoker. I smoked a pack to two packs a day for quite a long time. The last time I saw my Mr. Blue alive he was a frail and frightened man, barely sixty years old, moving slowly through a thickly carpeted house with a small tank of oxygen in tow. Mr. Blue had smoked most of his adult life. He had come of age in a time when there were no Surgeon General's warnings, few "No Smoking" signs, and no nonsmoking sections in restaurants. By the time of my last visit he had developed severe emphysema and was so terrified of an attack that he refused to part from his emergency oxygen for even a moment. He died a few months later. Over the years he had tried to quit smoking many times unsuccessfully. Every time I think about having a cigarette nowadays, Mr. Blue enters my mind. Mr. Blue, strong and healthy, up on a ladder in white overalls painting the hospital. Mr. Blue filling the minibike's tank with gas. Mr. Blue laughing and casting his line into the lake. Mr. Blue coughing and sick in his kitchen.

I haven't had a cigarette in three years.

yesterday, tomorrow, and today

If not now, when?

—HILLEL

Each day I have to suit up and show up for my journey. But it's hard to move forward when I have one foot stuck in yesterday and the other foot stuck in tomorrow.

As long as we live, the future will come. Be it good or bad. We will always have yesterday to think about. Good or bad. But the quality of our journeys will ultimately be determined by how we travel today. It seems simple, but unfortunately this is a hard lesson to remember. Some days, worrying about the mistakes I made yesterday or what bad things might happen tomorrow makes me so sad I want to hide from today. I just can't seem to get the get-up-and-go it takes to suit up and show up. So, a long time ago, whenever I found myself living in yesterday or tomorrow, I started calling myself back to today. I called out to myself: "GregAlan, come back. Come back, GregAlan." It didn't matter if I was walking down the street. Saying this to myself reminded me that I needed to pay attention to that day's journey. Calling myself back reminded me to stay in the *"now."* I even called myself back from pleasant thoughts if those thoughts rested too long in the past or the future because I didn't want to get stuck. Thoughts about an upcoming party or a check I was expecting in the mail were pleasant thoughts but they were pleasant thoughts for tomorrow, not for today. For sure it's fine to think about tomorrow. It's important to make plans for our journey. But we need to stay mostly in today because that's the day we're journeying in.

A friend of mine in Chicago used to have this old broken-down sports car that he swore he'd get running one day. The body was rusted through in a few places. The convertible top was hanging in shreds. Several essential parts were missing from the engine. In fact none of Nick's friends had ever known the car to even start. It just sat quietly on the street in front of Nick's house waiting for the junkman. Nonetheless, Nick swore that one day he would be riding around in that old car.

One day Nick asked me to give him a lift over to a repair shop on Chicago's south side.

"Whatcha goin' out there for?" I asked as we rode along in my green Chevy pickup.

"Gotta give this mechanic some money for workin' on my car," Nick answered, gazing out the passenger window.

"What car?"

"My sports car," Nick replied matter-of-factly.

I kind of laughed under my breath, and Nick smiled. We talked about everything else except that sports car until we got to the junkyard/repair shop. Nick hopped out and then was back in a flash.

"When's it gonna be ready?" I asked, trying to keep a straight face.

"When it's ready," Nick grinned, slapping me on the shoulder.

I must've carried Nick out to that junkyard five or six times over the next year. Other friends did too.

"You seen Nick?" somebody would ask.

"Yeah. I just took him out to pay some money on his car," another friend would reply. And all of us who knew about Nick and that car would kind of chuckle and shake our heads.

Week after week, month after month, Nick carried a little money out to that mechanic to cover labor or buy a part. And then one day I was standing in front of a barbecue joint called Lem's on Seventy-sixth Street and a little green sports car zoomed to a halt at the curb in front of me. At first Nick didn't even look my way. Then ever so slowly his head began to turn in my direction, all the while the grin on his face getting bigger and bigger. Nick never said a word, he just looked at me and nodded with that wide grin on his face. Nick wasn't alone either, he had three ladies with him in that teeny-tiny car. One of the women, LaDonna, was a buddy of ours. LaDonna had known all about

Nick's many pilgrimages to the repair shop, and as she knelt in the back of that car where no passenger was ever intended to ride, all she could do was shrug her shoulders and laugh. And still, Nick wasn't saying a word. He was just grinnin' from ear to ear.

From the moment I first started hanging out with Nick he used to talk to me about making my journey one day at a time and living life in the now. The day Nick pulled up in that old car was the day I finally understood what ''living life in the now'' meant.

Nick's car was brought back to life one part at a time, one trip out to the repair place at a time, one day at a time. Then one day, after many individual days of effort, Nick realized his goal, and came driving up in his little green sports car.

It may seem that the most important part of our journey is our destination. That the value of the race lies only at the finish line. Remember, however, that each step we take in the race, each stride up the mountain, makes us stronger and wiser. And each stride takes us closer to our destination. Ultimately, it is the attention to each step that will get us where we're going. A mountain climber may mark the summit as his destination. But it is his attention to every little foothold along the way that will get him safely to the top. Or, imagine an astronaut on his way to the moon never looking out the window. Sure he'll get to the moon but think of all the wonderful sights he'll miss on the way. There is much to enjoy as we travel. Adversity and struggle will not lie in every step of our journey. Fun, beauty, love, and rest can also strengthen our hearts and our minds and make us better Warriors.

All of us have places we want to go. Things we want to see and do. So, gentlemen, concentrate on each step you take toward those destinations. If you want a nice-looking car or a college education, focus your energies on the steps you must take "today" to get to your destinations. As you take today's steps, look around. See what you can see. Find out what there is to enjoy and to learn from each step of your journey.

A baby doesn't get mad or give up when he discovers that he can't just jump out of his crib and walk. For goodness' sakes, if the child just sat down with his mouth stuck out thinking about the big day when he would take his first steps, he'd never walk! So, you check out a baby. Shorty will scoot, crawl, or whatever he can to get where he's goin'. And while he's traveling he's having big fun. I know he is because most of the time he's laughin' while he's crawlin' and getting into everything. Just crawling here and there. Tearin' stuff up. The child knows that walking is possible. He really wants to walk too, just like those folks he sees up on two legs all the time. Still, he has a great time while he's crawling. In fact most of his energy is focused on crawling somewhere he can enjoy getting into something. Then one day, Shorty gets up. He's shaky, but he gets up. But just like that he falls and busts his big baby head. Sometimes he even laughs when he busts it. You've seen babies fall; first thing that hits the floor is that big ol' head. *Pow!* Everybody's lookin', mouths wide open. Everybody's thinkin', "Baby got to be dead.'' Mama's screamin'. Daddy's on the run. Then just as Daddy reaches down to scoop the baby into his arms, the baby looks up and laughs, wearing a look that says, ''Gee, that hurt a little bit but I bet I looked real funny falling. Wanna see it again?'' Babies can find joy in their lives even before they reach the destination of walking. Sometimes babies can even find something to laugh at when their journey hurts a little. And so can we.

There's joy and there is pain on our journey. Travel in the now. Focus on each step and eventually you will find yourself at your destination. Like my friend A.L. always says, ''Never mind the destination, just enjoy the ride!''

Maybe that's why whenever I drove Nick out to that junkyard he was always smiling.

silence

When the heart speaks, the tongue is silent.
—AFRICA

When I was a teenager my mother would occasionally suggest that I "go somewhere and reflect." What she meant was that perhaps I should sit down and take some time to just be quiet and think. I laughed the first few times she suggested this, but after hearing it so many times it just made me mad. "Reflect on what?" I asked.

"I don't know," she'd say. "Just reflect."

This would make me even madder. "How am I supposed to do this reeeeeflect, stuff?" I would smirk.

"I don't know, but I think you just need to reflect for a while."

And with that, Mom would send me to my room to commence an extended period of reeeeflection!

As I sat angrily in my room I would think: "This is really stupid. I've got to sit here doing nothing while a whole buncha stuff is goin' on in the world. People playin' ball, listening to music, dancing, talking to girls, goin' to the movies, and I'm sittin' here like an idiot, *reflecting.*"

Long before Mom began suggesting I "go somewhere and reflect," I had come to believe that silence and being quiet were tools of authority. If a lot of kids were caught talking in class or disobeying the rules, the teacher might call for a quiet time. Even in kindergarten, an afternoon of wild fun was always cut short by the mandatory nap time, a time when the rules of no talking, giggling, or humming were strictly enforced. Throughout my school years I knew that I was supposed to be quiet in class, quiet in church, very often quiet around the house, on the bus, in the car, and on and on and on. For me, being quiet most often meant not having any fun.

The longer I am on this journey the more important silence has become. Maybe it's because I'm older now and I'm ready for a pipe and rocking chair, but I don't think so. In fact I believe that if I had understood more about the usefulness of silence I would have come to cherish its clarifying power as a much younger man.

Silence helps me see myself and my journey much clearer.

When I am silent my energy seems to transfer from my mouth and my ears to my eyes—my mind's eye. In my silence I am better able to step away from myself and see myself as I really am or how I would like to be. In my silence I can often see people and situations in a clearer and more peaceful way—free of anger and resentment. When I withdraw from the rock, roll, and rap of life for a little while, I am better able to see how to make my journey among the rock, the roll, and the rap. Between TV, billboards, radio, newspapers, and magazines my mind is flooded with information—*buy this, wear that, look this way, look that way, go here, go there, say this, say that.* By the end of the day my mind is overcrowded. Sometimes it feels as if I'm an android responding automatically to what's going on around me. When I step away to a quiet place and just sit and maybe focus on a flower, an insect, maybe even a building, those messages that have been invading my brain all day have a chance to float away. What remains are the really important things that I need to reflect on. In the silence it's easier for those important things to connect with G.O.D. And for me, when that connection is made, the answers come, and the path for my journey becomes clearer.

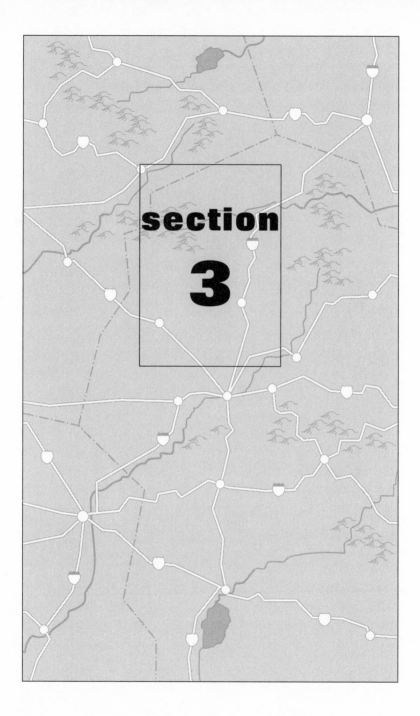

section

3

momma, angels, and ''ho's''

That I will be free to be who I will be,
free to become whatever my life requires
of me, without posturing,
without compromise, without terror.

That my son, who is a Black man,
and that I, a Black woman, may keep faith
with each other, and with those others
whom we may have the privilege
to serve, and to join.

—JUNE JORDAN

Throughout my boyhood a woman was my primary protector and teacher. Today I can honestly say that Georgia Faye Travis was also my best and most devoted friend. But be assured, gentlemen, that this was not an understanding that I carried with me as a boy, or even as a young man.

Until I was seven, when we bought our first car, Mom and I would ride the bus wherever we wanted to go, except when we went to the laundromat. For that we used our legs and my red wagon. The dirty clothes went in the baskets and me and the baskets went into the wagon that mother pulled behind her for ten or twelve blocks to the laundromat. Other, longer trips required bus tokens, well-pressed clean clothes, brushed hair, and pastel green snowsuits in winter.

Mom worked as a nurse during the years before I started school. Every morning we'd ride the bus together to our individual destinations. My stop was first: a small in-home day care half a block from the bus stop just up a low hill. Georgia would set me off the bus and urge me to hurry up the hill. The driver always delayed his journey just long enough to give Mom time to see me safely on my way. He'd pull away slowly with the door still open and Mom watching and/or hollering at me. "Hurry up! Get up there, Greggie. Go on!" By the time the bus passed out of sight I was knocking on the lowest portion of the gray aluminum screen door just as a woman (her smile is all I can remember) opened the door and the warm smell of oatmeal and butter smacked me in the face.

One of my most vivid memories of my mother as a protector comes from a cold winter morning when I waddled up the hill in my thick pastel green snowsuit through snow so deep that each step brought a bulky insulated knee almost to my chin.

The snowsuit's hood was tied tightly around my face over a wool knit cap so all I could see to the left or to the right was the inside of that hood. But I could hear, and what I heard sounded like an animal.

In order to determine the source of the barking and growling which seemed to be getting closer, I stopped in the nearly waist-high snow and swung my head to the left. "Yep, that's what I thought," I said to myself. "A dog."

For every Sunday without fail Mom had drilled me with manila colored flash cards. The words on the cards were pretty simple: two-, three-, and four-letter words like "it," "car," "look," and things like that. At three years old I hated those Sunday afternoon flash cards. I wanted to go out in the yard and play, or run my train set, or something. But on that day on that hill in that thick, sweaty, nearly-impossible-to-move-in snowsuit, three words from that set of flash cards went off like beacons in my head: BIG, DOG, and RUN! I screamed as I turned toward the safety of the day care only a few yards ahead, and with my first fleeing step I fell flat on my face. And just as I started to raise myself out of the snow—*Wham!*—those mighty paws landed smack on my back. The growling was in my ears now. I could almost feel the beast's hot breath and slobber through the back of my snowsuit. "He's trying to get my neck!" my head cried.

Hoping that snowsuits were to dogs what "the covers" were to the bogeyman, I rolled up in a ball and tried not to move. You see, all kids know that if you stay perfectly still under

the covers the bogeyman can't even touch you, let alone eat
you. But I could feel this bogeyman—or bogeydog—pawing at
my snowsuit and poking me with its snout. I heard its hungry
sniffing and deadly growl. And at that moment I knew with the
utmost certainty that it was going to eat me. "Mommaaa! Mom-
maaaaaa!"

No sooner had the call for help left my lips than she
was there. Never has John Wayne or Wesley Snipes arrived in a
nickier nick of time. "No! Get away! Get *away!*" Momma
screamed, flinging her arms wildly at my hungry tormentor.

In an instant the animal leapt from my back and turned to
face the woman who dared to interfere with his breakfast. The
dog snarled and showed its pointed yellow teeth. Mother yelled,
"No!" and lunged at the dog. I was on my back watching this
test of wills at the exact moment my mother lunged. I heard the
German shepherd yelp frightfully and run away, leaving blurred,
hurried tracks through the fresh front yard snow. Yep, my mom
was always a good protector.

As a little boy, say up to the age of eight or nine, I also considered Momma a pretty good buddy. Most of her time away from
the downtown glove factory where she worked was spent with
me. We laughed a lot. We danced in the living room sometimes.
We carried blankets and sandwiches to the park. And, believe it
or not, we even talked at night, bedroom to bedroom, just like
that TV family the Waltons.

By the time I was fourteen Georgia had saved enough money to buy a small three-bedroom house. Up till then I slept on a single wooden bed in the dining room of our rented house at 1534 Cleveland. Almost every night it seemed, I'd ask a whole bunch of questions about one thing or another and Georgia would do her best to give me some answers. Sometimes when I asked a nighttime question there'd be a long pause. I thought then that maybe she had fallen asleep so I'd call to her, "Momma?"

"Yeah?" she'd say flatly, just to let me know she had heard me.

And then I'd ask my question again.

During the very early years of my boyhood when Georgia and I were first learning about each other, if she didn't answer one of my nightly questions immediately, I'd interrupt the first few seconds of her silence with a few "Huh, Mom? Huh, Mom?"'s. Over the years we got to know each other pretty well and on those nights when the answers were slow in coming I'd just kind of let my need to know lean patiently in the doorway between our sleeping places until she was ready.

"Well, I'll tell ya," she'd begin slowly. "I'm not really sure, Greggie."

But I knew she was sure. She was just taking her time. Thinking about what she was going to say. The answer was coming soon. So I'd start getting ready. First I'd get really comfortable. Shift a little bit until I found just the right position and spot in the bed. Then I'd cross my ankles, place my palms behind my head, and stay real still. Even in the short distance between our rooms, the smallest rustle of pajamas, sheets, blankets, or even a bedspread could momentarily drown out a word or an inflection and spoil the map that Georgia would give me for my journey.

For instance, years before I began studying the Commodity Kid I would wonder about this strange boy who sat in the car in the backyard across the alley. And I'd wonder if Mom ever wondered about him as I did. "Mom," I'd whisper into the dark that separated our rooms, "do you think the guy who sits in the car across the alley is crazy?"

And then she'd begin, "Well, Greg, perhaps . . ." (her answers to the difficult questions usually began this way). To Momma, beginning her answer with "perhaps" was a way of letting me know that there might be other answers to consider beside hers. But to me, no matter how tentative or careful her response, Georgia's opinion was the absolute truth about "the way things are." You see it was this woman who taught me that two plus two equals four—and she was right. She told me that the stove was hot—and it was. She told me that she was the parent and I was the child and that she knew what was best for me. And although I didn't always like what she considered "best" for me, the comfort and happiness of our lives together taught me to believe her. Not to mention the abundance of food in my belly, the solid roof over my head, and the number of toys under my bed.

Even today the details about my mother's journey into womanhood are pretty sketchy. There are a few stories—ones about my grandfather, about growing up in Mississippi, about certain teachers, neighbors, and personalities who left an impression on her. But Mom has never been one for telling her "personal business" even to me. Nor is she a woman who talks much about her personal feelings or failures. Nonetheless, from the very beginning of our lives together she prepared many clear and detailed maps for my journey, maps so precise that even at this moment I am still following a path she began to show me when I was just two years old.

"And God stepped out on space, looked around, and said, 'I'm lonely, I'll make me a world.' "

The first few times I watched Mother deliver her version of James Weldon Johnson's "The Creation" in church I giggled because her voice was so much louder than I'd heard it around the house. It was strange to hear her speaking in such a big voice. A voice that made you jump at the first couple of words. A voice that could be heard all the way to the back of the church. She was magnificent, even though it was kinda funny to hear her voice the thoughts of God. Whenever she got to God's first line, "I'm lonely, I'll make me a world," she made it sound as if God was just some regular guy hanging out around heaven, bored. Then all of a sudden he gets this idea to make animals and people and stuff. I never really thought I'd be able to deliver it the way she did. I couldn't imagine how she memorized all those words, but I hoped one day I'd be able to talk just like her.

Within a few years of those first hearings I was mouthing the words with Mom from my seat among the other parishioners. I had heard her deliver this piece so many times I could anticipate nearly every one of her gestures and inflections. One day when I was about twelve Mother mentioned that someone from one of the local churches had asked her to deliver one of Johnson's sermons for a special service. When I asked her which one of the sermons she was going to do she told me she wasn't going to do any of them. "So whatcha gonna do, Mom, sing instead?"

"No. I'm not going to sing either. I thought perhaps you should do 'The Creation.'"

"Do what?" I replied, shocked.

"You heard me," came Momma's flat reply.

Despite my fears and protests my preparation began. "The Creation" was the most extensive piece of prose I had set out to memorize. It was long and difficult and there was also interpretation to consider: vocal inflections and gestures. Mom and I worked for a week or so until that Sunday afternoon when I took my place before the congregation of a local Baptist church. There wasn't much originality in my delivery. I gave the piece pretty much as I had heard her give it so many wonderful times. When I finished the kind folks applauded, nodded their heads, said lots of "Amens," and even threw in a few "Praise-the-

Lords." When the mistress of ceremonies stood to thank me and introduce the next gospel performer she said something about "teaching a child in the way he should go."

Today, each time I step in front of the camera in the hope of creating a believable character, I go back to the map Mom gave me in our living room workshop. I go back automatically to her teaching and use it like an atlas to help give direction to my performance. I don't remember my first recitation, but according to Georgia I was two years old. The recitation was at least three quarters of a page and I recited it before the entire congregation of the New Jerusalem Church of God in Christ entirely from memory. In 1976 I walked into a theater in St. Paul, Minnesota, and landed my first full-time acting job with the city's first professional African-American Theater Company. I had never taken a formal acting class. Instead the skill and confidence I took with me to that audition came from those many days and evenings in Momma's living room when she would demonstrate how a single voice could bring the written word to life. Today, whenever I write a check at the grocery store, I know that the food I've placed in my basket is there in large measure because of the maps Georgia gave me so many years ago.

The gift of my vocation is just one example of the maps I got from Mom. As a boy, however, it was impossible for me to see how these maps would actually serve me as a man. Even though when I looked about at the men around me I saw that few were as talented or perhaps even as bright as my mother, yet it appeared to me that there was a distinct difference in status between women and men.

Momma had "skills." She was smart, pretty, talented, self-sufficient, proud, and poor. All around me there were other women, some with skills and some not, some with children and some not; most were simply doing the best they could with what they had. All were women who were for the most part poor, powerless, and struggling. By contrast, most of the men I observed always had twenty dollars for the church collection plate. The men I saw immediately outside my environment, the ones in movies and television documentaries, were warriors, travelers, discoverers of distant lands, conquerors of powerful enemies. Consequently I came to see men as rulers of nations and builders of great civilizations. In my young world—the world of girls and women—females worked mundane jobs, cooked and cleaned, cared for children, taught songs in Sunday school, prayed and cried for "fast" daughters, fallen fathers, lost sons, and a sweeter life in the next world. I loved Momma dearly. She was my teacher, my protector, and my advocate, but I did not want her condition. I wanted desperately to separate myself from her, her difficulties, her poverty, and her sadness. It was clear to me women bore both great beauty and great burden. As I journeyed I would come to covet and worship one and dutifully avoid the other.

My models of manhood were fashioned mostly by the men I saw at church, Mr. Blue, and the heroic men I saw on television and in the movies. The men at church were great guys:

responsible, respectful, courteous, listened to and attended to by the women. But words of faith from a woman to the congregation were called "teaching," and identical words from a man were called "preaching." And even though the meaning and intent of the teaching and preaching might be the same and be given on the same day, women's "teachings" were never ever heard from the pulpit but only from the floor *beneath* the preacher's podium. And at church dinners the men, children, and elders always ate first. Often, the women who had prepared the food never came to table at all, but instead appeared comfortable nibbling from plates within the confines of the kitchen.

Mr. Blue was a hard worker, a hunter, a fisherman, and every two years or so he traded for a new car. He had style and was quick with a joke or a funny piece of poetry. He was forever going around reciting some poem about a boy on a burning deck "eating peanuts by the peck." He'd actually stand in the middle of the floor, place one hand on his chest, stretch the other arm out toward an invisible audience (usually me and Mom), and raise his voice as if he was trying to be heard in the back row. "The boy stood on the burning deck! Eating peanuts by the peck!" (I don't recall exactly, but he never seemed to get any further than those first two lines. But even now, as I write about it, I smile.) Mr. Blue's delivery, however, never came close to Mom's.

Likewise the guys on TV and in the movies were strong, brave, smart, and tough. I thought most of the guys I saw around me were pretty cool too. Pretty good "men" as far as I could tell. But there was, of course, a certain distance between us because all I really knew of these men was what I saw on the outside. So I set about patterning my own manly image based primarily on male exteriors I saw from a distance: to me, a man dressed well and drove a nice car, a man was kind to women and children, a man showed respect for, and faith in, God; and he did so quietly, with a small nod and a deep-throated "Amen." A true man hunted and ate what he killed from the woods and fished from the rivers and lakes. A real man shot pheasants out of the field and sky. A real man always kept money, and, perhaps most importantly, a girlfriend . . . or two.

All around me men were getting their goodies now. Savoring the best and most exciting that life had to offer. And perhaps chief among those pleasures was women themselves! Even at the age of ten two things were crystal clear: like kings, men ruled! Women suffered and served—on television, in business, in politics, in love, and in war. This shallow view of women I derived simply from the world around me; at ten years old my perspective on women was as narrow as the confines of my own experience. As I studied the history books I was given at school I could only conclude that women, while noble and compassionate beings, would be encouraged or allowed to rise only so far, and rarely any higher than second position to the left and slightly to the rear of a man. It was clear: opportunity, success, and a better life depended upon my becoming one of the boys. I too wanted *my* sweetness now! Therefore, I was willing to subscribe to almost anything or anyone that would teach me the ways of men.

Mr. Blue was both a Mason and a Shriner. For years I can remember him carrying around these small black books in the breast pocket of his white overalls. Often he'd sit on the living room ottoman studying the text through his paint-speckled lenses. Once or twice I tried to peek over his shoulder. Both times the tiny book would be slammed shut instantly as Mr. Blue turned his head to look over his shoulder with his eyes cut real tight to the corners of their sockets; he'd not say a word until I went on about my business.

Every now and then Mr. Blue would stand in our living room and recite a few words from one of the books in grave tones. The words sounded official and important. When I asked their meaning Mr. Blue would just scowl and slip the book back into his pocket. When Mom heard him go on like that she just rolled her eyes and "Harumphed" as if it was all silliness. But I believed it was anything but silly.

One day Mr. Blue literally jumped through our front door at 1534 Cleveland. He was grinning and kind of doing a happy little dance on his toes between the living room and the dining room. I heard him announce to my mother that he was now a "thirty-third." Then he positioned himself in the center of the dining room a couple of feet from my bed and recited some more of those official-sounding words. When I asked both of them what was going on, Mom explained that Mr. Blue was

now a thirty-third-degree Mason. I knew that this had something to do with one of those little books he was always studying
out of. I also knew that the Masons were a group of men who
had secrets, and a secret place where they met, and that they
gave dances for teenagers at a local hall called the Brotherhood
and the Sisterhood. On many Fridays at about six o'clock Mr.
Blue would take me with him to the Brotherhood and I'd hang
out while he loaded cases of soda into a cooler and placed hot
dogs and links in a boiling pot of water. Sometimes teenage girls
and boys would show up early and hang around laughing and
talking just outside the hall's door waiting for the dance to begin. Even at ten my curiosity about the secrets of Mr. Blue and
his Masons paled in comparison to my curiosity about the
secrets of those teenage girls chewing gum and wearing lipstick
on the steps of the Brotherhood hall.

Not long after the day Mr. Blue came dancing through our
door I came to understand that a Mason of the thirty-third degree was the highest kind of Mason you could ever be. Soon I
decided that one day I too would become a Mason of the thirty-
third degree. Mr. Blue told me that you couldn't just sign up
and join the Masons but that someone had to bring you in and
say you were okay, and that you deserved to be among these
most knowledgeable and honorable of men. I actually used to
have dreams about being brought into the secret place by Mr.
Blue himself. In these dreams I saw myself studying secrets from
little books and cutting my eyes at strangers seeking forbidden
tastes of ancient knowledge. I saw myself selling soda pop and

hot dogs to teenagers at Friday night dances, enjoying (like Mr. Blue) the respect and admiration of young people. Today I don't know much about the Masons, though I've heard good and bad. No matter. Still today the title of thirty-third-degree Mason for me is synonymous with the title of thirty-third-degree ''man.'' Even the fact that Mr. Blue verbally and physically abused my mother before finally almost killing her does not, even as I write, keep me from crying as I recall that man, and the great promise of my membership in the fraternal order of Masons. Today there are other fraternities with secret languages, secret scripts, and secret places where none but the initiated may enter. To become one of these a boy must be brought in. Someone must vouch for his qualifications, character, and willingness to become part of the order. And even though members of the fraternity and the fraternity itself might be of questionable character, a lot of young guys are in such desperate need of a sponsor, a place to be among men, a place where they can find help in defining their own manhood, that they become willing to ignore the truth in order to preserve a place for themselves among a brotherhood of men. In my case I chose to betray my mother by demeaning and disrespecting others of her gender rather than risk losing my place with the fellas.

For me the military was the only place I could be certain to learn the ways of men. By age thirteen or so I had become convinced that the ways of men were manifest in the ways of war. In seventh grade I asked Mother to send me to a military high school or academy. After telling me point blank that there was no way she could afford private school tuition she suggested that I pick up *Lovejoy's Guide to Prep Schools and Military Academies*, choose a "nonmilitary" boarding school, and see if I couldn't secure a scholarship to attend. I knew she wasn't serious and I thought no more about it. Of course a few weeks later she brought it up again. When I scoffed at the notion that I could win a scholarship to a private school she pulled rank and softly informed me that I would, at the very least, make the effort. The following fall after several handwritten letters and completed forms I began my ninth-grade year at one of our nation's oldest and most respected all-male institutions, Campion Jesuit High School, in Prairie du Chien, Wisconsin.

Once a month the school bused in Catholic schoolgirls from Dubuque or even Minneapolis for dances. Most of the month, however, the nearest black females were the dozen or so at Wylusing Academy across the railroad tracks from Campion. Among the boys of Campion the girls of Wylusing, black or otherwise, were rarely referred to as girls or young women. From the moment I learned of their existence they were most always referred to as the "Wylusing Ho's," as in "Hole," a derogatory word originally used to describe a prostitute. Even the guys at Campion who had girlfriends at Wylusing called them "Ho's." To my knowledge, not one of the Wylusing girls was or had ever been a prostitute. My understanding was that they had been sent to the school because they had gotten in trouble in their own school back home. Some of the Wylusing girls were awfully cute. Many had a great knack for humor. And God bless them, they were always sweet to me. From what I could see, some really loved a few of the older Campion brothers. There was one girl in particular, a little older than I was. I don't remember her name, but man oh man. I remember sitting in the student lounge staring at her the way you might stare at an angel if you ever got to see one. I swear all she was missing was wings. Sometimes when the guys would be sitting around talking among themselves and that word, ''Ho,'' would get to flying back and forth across the room, I'd think of her. Each time I said it, each time I heard it, I felt so bad. After a while, though, the word became easier to say and hear. You see in time I sort of built up calluses on my ears and brain. Now that I think about it they probably developed on my heart as well.

At fourteen, I saw girls as pretty amazing human beings. I still thought Mom was pretty amazing too, although, at that age, I never would have told her so. Certainly the girls at Wylusing were not like my mom, but they were still females and in my personal opinion they were as okay, if not better, than the guys. In my life, a woman had been my teacher, protector, provider, and primary companion for a long time. As a result, I held her, and most women in high esteem. The unmistakable signature of my own experience had shown me that women were at the very least the equal of men. At Campion I chose, however, to ignore the map of my own experience. It took me a while, but I got comfortable with calling those Wylusing women ''Ho's,'' even though every time I said it the word sounded like a cannon going off in my ears. I may have even flinched a little every time the word came out of my mouth. I ignored the truth of my own experience because somewhere in my head I mistakenly believed that term and other derogatory terms like it were passwords that would get me into the secret clubhouse of manhood. I thought they were required of any who belonged in the fraternity of men. Without a doubt I could have referred to the young women of Wylusing Academy in a respectful manner, not been ostracized by the Campion brothers, and still become a man to boot! And perhaps a better man at that. But the brothers were cool. Most of the black students were from big cities and to me big cities meant hip. Yup, I was in the midst of cool, hip, wanna-be powerful men like myself. Wanna-be-men, who, in casual conversation, called women ''Ho's'' with absolutely no respect whatsoever for the young women's personal character. You can bet I've never called Mom a ''Ho.'' But I used the word at Campion and I've used it a thousand times since in reference to both women I've known and women I've never met. Gentlemen, lots of us have been reared and are being reared by women. For years we depended upon them for our very lives. We've come to know these women as worthy and resourceful beings. We've also come to know that, traditionally, in our society, those same women are often relegated to secondary positions in relation to men. They may be the queens, but we are the kings! I betrayed my mother when I began to participate in that inequitable tradition. I perpetuated a bad thing in our culture, first in my speech, then, eventually, with my attitude. Maybe that's part of the reason we're always so quick to fight when somebody talks about our mom or our sister. Most of us will slap somebody in a minute for disrespecting Mom and sis. Could it be that somewhere inside we know that we have disrespected our own mothers and sisters when we disrespected other men's mothers, sisters, and daughters. That when we slap that other guy we slap him partly to slap the guilt out of our own heads?

When the boys of Campion talked about the girls of Wylusing, it was with the understanding that those girls were "oh, so very fine." It was also understood that generally speaking those girls were weak, not too bright, and primarily good only for sex. At fourteen, while I knew that girls were nice to look at, I knew hardly anything at all about sex. Yet I accepted and began to carry this negative attitude about women without having any personal experience to support such an attitude. The fellas at Campion shared the maps of their so-called experience with women but I never bothered to study those maps closely. I never bothered to cross-reference the information on those maps with the map of my own experience or someone else's map to see if the information I got from the guys at Campion was accurate. I never even bothered to check the information against my *feelings*. Earlier on, although I felt bad about calling girls "Ho's," not once did I sit down and reflect on how *I* felt when I said the word "Ho." If I had, perhaps some G.O.D. would have slipped inside my head and I might have found a way to hold on to my "groove"—my own idea of what was honorable and right.

. . .

Perhaps the very first thing I learned about girls was that they were made of sugar and spice and everything nice. It's no wonder then that as a teenager practically every young woman I spent any kind of time with turned out to be a disappointment. No matter how much sugar a person is made of there is absolutely no way they can be sweet twenty-four-seven. However, when I initially began paying attention to girls, my first opinion of the gender was that they were all, for the most part, angels. Angels were nice. Angels were kind. And above all, angels were perfect and *beautiful*. In my young eyes there were, of course, some little girls who appeared more angelic than others, but my overall view was that I (a boy) was a little beast and that they (girls) were little beauties. Like most boys, I grew up believing that one day I would marry and my wife "should" be beautiful. So very early on in my journey I began to measure a girl's entire character by how she looked. If from a distance I saw a girl who, according to my eyes, looked like an angel, my heart would light up instantly. "Surely," I'd say to myself, "she will be the sweetest, kindest, and smartest woman I'll ever meet!"

Having come to that conclusion, I would be in love before I crossed the street. After a few hours, days, or, if I was lucky, a few weeks, my "love" would wither from disappointment. "She's so lovely," I would think to myself. "How could she be so . . . so much like everybody else?" In other words, how could this "angel" be so human? For many years my expecta-

tions of women were so high (heavenly in fact) that I was subject to feeling ''let down'' by practically anything a girl did or
said. By the time I graduated from high school my vision of girls
as angels was still intact, but altered a bit by reality; to me, most
''beautiful'' women were still angels but they didn't realize they
were angels. So while I continued to *treat* women as if they were
angels I no longer expected their behavior to be eternally angelic.

Take a second and think about what it might be like to
actually meet a real-live girl angel from heaven. Man. I'd probably sit and stare at her for hours. I bet there would be this
yellow-white glow all around her. Her face would be perfect.
All of her features would be like something out of a painter's
imagination. She'd be smiling, of course. And sweet. Always
sweet, loving, gentle. A real angel would never get angry or raise
her voice. Of course she wouldn't be interested in guys because
angels don't do things like that. An angel, being an angel, would
watch over us as we went on our journey. She would comfort us
and keep us safe as we traveled. Our angel would journey with
us everywhere we went. That's an angel's duty, you know, to
watch over us as we go on our journey. It's an angel's responsibility to serve and to be happy and content in that service.

Well, if that's anything near what a real angel is like, then,
gentlemen, girls and women are no angels. I'd be more inclined
to say that women are beautifully and simply human beings.
Journeypersons like ourselves. Women are not made of either
sugar or spice. They are flesh and blood, capable of both great

compassion and great selfishness. When we measure women by angelic standards they are bound to let us down. The greatest difficulty, however, is that when we place women on a heavenly pedestal or seek to cage them as sweet and precious possessions, we do not view them or treat them as equals.

R. Kelly had a song out a while back where he was telling some girl, "You remind me of my jeep. You look just like my car." Let's take a look at that idea: R. Kelly loves his jeep. Great. His jeep looks good. Runs good. The jeep is R. Kelly's beautiful possession. The jeep's primary responsibility is to take R. Kelly where he wants to go and when. The jeep's job is to serve R. Kelly. To carry him on his journey. Clearly, women are not like jeeps. A woman's first responsibility is to get herself where she's going and when. A woman may look good but her "good looks" are not just for us to put on display for the fellas. Women are not property. They are not our pretty possessions.

How we see and think about women are very important. I believe that Mr. Blue's failure to see my mother as a fellow journeyperson on a path comparable to his, no higher and no lower, may have led him to hurt her physically. You hear about things like that on the news all the time. Some guy who used to go with some girl tracks her down, trying everything he can to get her to come back on his journey with him. Sounds like R. Kelly after someone stole his jeep, doesn't it? When the woman refuses to go because she wants to continue on her own journey the man may beat or even kill her. Perhaps he becomes enraged and violent because he believes that he has been betrayed. It is, after all, an "angel's" duty to accompany a man on his journey. Just as it is a jeep's responsibility to take us where we want to go. The notion of angels or jeeps going off by themselves, living their own lives, and dreaming their own dreams is ridiculous and unnatural. How dare they?

When we begin a relationship with a woman by putting her on a pedestal, she will inevitably fall. And once an angel falls where does she land? Does she land on the same level as ordinary men? Or does she fall to a status well beneath us. The fact that our angel has fallen from such heights will almost certainly mean that her image, in our eyes, will suffer some damage. The more the women around me fell, the more aware I became that women were not angels. As they fell, I became willing to view women not as ordinary people but as beings who had fallen from grace—angels who had been kicked off their heavenly pedestals because they were unworthy. Whether our view of women is high or low, whether we view them as angels or "Ho's," any view that sees women as unequal to men is equally dangerous to us. While I have never actually believed that women are not as smart as men or as worthy as men, my conversation about Campion should tell you that I was more than willing to speak of women as if they were less intelligent and less worthy. Negative names for women encourage negative views of women. For years white folks referred to African-Americans as niggers. The word nigger helped reinforce negative and violent attitudes toward black folks. Black people weren't called "Nigger People" or "Nigger Human Beings," they were just simply niggers—no humanity involved. Germans were Germans. French were French. White folks were at least "folks." But nigger meant "nothing," nonhuman. I've never heard of the "Ho People." Where are they from? A "Ho," like a nigger, is a nothing, nonhuman. Most often, in order for us to hurt others, we must first dehumanize them. Make them subhuman, of less value than ourselves. The Nazis did it by teaching people that Jews were subhuman and not the equal of non-Jews. America did it by convincing itself that the millions of Africans it enslaved and murdered were property and not people (sort of a nation of "jeeps," if you will). Gentlemen, it is extremely difficult to do physical violence to other human beings when you view them as equals—as beings with dignity. But it becomes amazingly easy to harm others when we strip them of their dignity and their equality. Once we begin to refer to women as bitches and "Ho's" we are not only encouraging violence against women, but we may be only a few steps away from physically abusing women ourselves.

Gentlemen, women are travelers just like us. Mothers, sisters, aunts, girlfriends, lovers, and wives are on a road just like we are. Be a man of honor; don't be an obstacle in a journeywoman's path. And beware of placing obstacles in your own path. You can't just go around slapping women upside the head because they say something you don't like. You can't just put your hands on a woman because you want to. You can't just snatch a woman because you feel like it. And if you do feel like snatching her, talk to somebody about that feeling before you snatch her. Suit up and show up somewhere and share the map of your "feelings" with another human being. Make an effort to find some G.O.D. (You better ask somebody!) The penalties for abuse are severe because the damage done by abuse is severe. The bottom line is this: verbal and physically abusive behavior toward women may build an obstacle in your path that will be difficult if not impossible for you to climb.

Mother taught me the basics of being a good and honorable human being. And she set some mighty hard boundaries. But when I began to look for a model of manhood and found that for all her teaching and love she and her gender were considered second-class figures in the world I began to resent her boundaries and the authority she held over me. After all, I was a prince destined to be king. I was going to become a Mason! And she was a member of the "weaker sex." A queen perhaps, but ultimately a woman and subject to the authority of kings. At thirteen I started trying to sever my ties to my mother so I could begin my ascension to the throne of manhood. This process of separation, the professionals tell me, is quite natural and necessary as we get closer to becoming men. I, however, began this process in utter panic, terrified that because of the closeness of my relationship with my mother I was somehow at risk of not crossing over into the world of men as other boys did. My fear was caged in rage and viciousness so ugly I hardly understand how my mother endured it. I began by telling Mother that I hated her; that I didn't want to be seen with her in public; that I was ashamed of her and tired of my friends' sincere greeting, "Hey, Greg, what's up? Where's your mom?"

My homeys weren't trying to be funny. It was simply that for most of my young life my mother and I were always together. She left me with baby-sitters only during the week while she was working. On weekends she took me along to her second job in a nearby nursing home. We shopped together. We attended church together. We went to the movies together just as children and their parents do. But at thirteen I feared that continuing this togetherness would almost certainly condemn me to share in her second-class status. I felt I had to get out, get up, and get on as quickly as possible before it was too late. Even though I had little idea where I was headed when I began to break away—there was really no one I trusted to guide me toward manhood. Oddly enough, however, as I ridiculed my mother and sought out the world of men, most often it was women I latched on to as my rite of passage into that world. Time and time again I eased in alongside a woman on her journey believing that our travels together would take me into manhood.

About the same time as I was telling Mother I hated her I was beginning to discover other women who demanded much less of me than she did. Journeywomen with broad beautiful hips and different kinds of boundaries. Girls who smiled when I looked at them. Females who whispered, "I love you," in the dark. Women who called me their "man." Women who let me touch them as a man. The love and approval of these women seemed much easier to earn than my mother's love and approval. They cared less about whether I did well in school or practiced piano. And what's more, some of these women had been deceived as thoroughly as I had. They had been taught their traditional place was as objects for sex and display. Often, despite the reality of their own abilities and experiences these women accepted themselves as weaker and not quite as capable as men. No matter how inept I was at being a man, those women and girls willingly and lovingly took a place (or pretended to take a place) behind me and my boyish ignorance. Chief among these confused angels was my beloved Simone.

I was angry when Simone first started talking to me as if she liked me. I had seen Simone around for a long time. I thought she was a lot older than I was because by the time we started talking she had a baby and grown guys were hitting on her all the time. When she gave me her phone number I thought she was just messin' with me because she had caught me looking at her legs in church one night. "Whatchu lookin' at?" she had said with an attitude as bright as the pretty gold tooth in her smile.

Simone had turned around just as I was leaning over the back of her pew to spy on those big, pretty, butterscotch thighs. Wham! Busted! That's all there was to it. I could either fight or flee. I fought.

"Them big legs. What you think I'm lookin' at?" I responded, truly expecting a slap.

There was a long pause during which my two fifteen-year-old partners, Larry and Carl, slid to the other end of the pew, out of reach. They were still sliding when Simone threw a counterpunch.

"You like what you see?" she said softly. Her face slipped from serious to a sexy fourteen-carat smile right in sync with the terrified surprise spreading across my own mug. "Well," she nudged. "What's the matter? Cat got your tongue?"

"Naw. I mean yeah! I mean . . . no . . . I . . . I . . . Yeah! Yeah! I like it. Yeah, I like it." I stated flatly. It was too late, though. She had me. "I should have quit while I was ahead," I thought to myself as Larry and ol' "no neck" Carl fanned themselves with church bulletins and discreetly laughed themselves silly. The ushers were passing the offering plates right about then and I hurried to make my getaway. After a few minutes pacing around outside trying to figure "How I let that girl embarrass me like that," that girl stepped right in my face.

"What's wrong with you?" she asked with a straight face.

I took a moment before looking up in order to get as much bass in my voice as possible before I spoke. "Why you wanna mess with me?" I asked as streetified as I could.

"I wasn't messin' with you. You was lookin'. I just wanted to know if you liked what you saw."

"So what if I did?" I responded quickly. I was trying to help Simone get to the punch line as fast as possible—the part where she would tell me how young I was and how unhip I was and how I ought not even think about it. *In your dreams, Gene!*

I pushed harder. "So what if I did like it?"

"Well, I guess that would be all right." This she said in the most gentle, womanly voice I had ever heard. I am sure now that Georgia had spoken to me like that many times when I was a little boy. But at fifteen it had been too long ago to remember. Perhaps Momma had stopped speaking to me in that voice when she realized how difficult it would be to bring a young boy into adulthood alone. Perhaps out of absolute necessity she had sacrificed gentleness for firm principles, solid skills, and boundaries. Nonetheless in 1971 at 7 P.M. on a Sunday, I rediscovered that gentleness on the steps of the Morning Star Baptist Church—let the church say, "Amen."

Simone ruled our relationship with that same almost invisible gentleness. She was only a year older than I, but even at sixteen she knew more about caring and commitment than I would come to know in the next twenty years. At the start it was Simone's journey and I was happy to go along. It was Simone who suggested activities and places to go. I didn't have a driver's license when we started going together, but Simone did. It seemed to me that she knew a lot more than I did about a lot of things. Simone knew how to be cool while sipping a wine cooler. Simone had grown-up sisters so she knew how to hang out with adults and not act like a kid. She knew a couple of nightclubs where underage kids could get in. Simone knew how to sing the Jesus songs and how to make the church get up on its feet and shout and cry. Simone knew just how to fix her hair, her face, and her eyes. She knew how to look at a boy, how to set her feelings in her eyes and let her eyes become mirrors—mirrors where I could catch long looks at the man I longed to be.

During the first six months of our relationship Simone was the leader since she was genuinely more mature and more aware of what she needed out of the relationship. Later, however, the responsibility of leadership seemed to shift. When we made plans to go out Simone began asking me to make the decisions. Often when I asked for her input she would simply say, "Oh, I don't care. Whatever you want to do." Unlike the early days of our dating I was more apt to scold her and playfully tell her what and what not to do. To my surprise, many times when I asked why she had not followed up on a particular idea or activity her response would be, "You told me not to." Whenever I heard this I was absolutely shocked. Simone was and still is an assertive, self-sufficient person. Nonetheless, my new role as decision maker and her occasional willingness to submit to my male authority made me feel mighty manly.

Simone and I once made love on a hillside for hours. I had been given an eleven o'clock curfew. Simone's was maybe one or two. Somewhere around midnight in the midst of our love-making Simone started to cry. When I paused she whispered something in my ear that changed my journey. "You make me feel so good," she cried softly. If naked butts could fly I would have floated all the way to the roof of the car. I looked at my watch several times that night. The hour grew later and later but I didn't care. When I walked through the front door of Georgia's house somewhere around seven in the morning neither Mom nor I said a word. She must have thought I was crazy. I offered no excuses, no pleas for forgiveness. I simply tossed her car keys on the coffee table and headed for my room. After all, a "man" didn't have to explain anything to anyone. I couldn't have explained it anyhow. But that night I believed that I had found a passage from the world of boys to the world of men. For a few incredible hours it seemed that I was as much a man as a man could be. I didn't need a sponsor nor someone to hold my hand as I went. I didn't need the Masons, the military, or Mr. Blue's help. I had Simone. Her eyes, her breasts, her smile would take me where I needed to go.

I closed the door to my room, lay down on the single bed I had slept in since I was seven, closed my eyes, and thought of Simone and the next time her love would make me a man.

It was with Simone that I began using women as a primary measure of my manhood. For me sex became a way of making sure I was "okay"—of feeling like a worthwhile person. Over time the faces of women became my mirror. If a woman smiled when I looked at her, I felt good about myself. If, when a woman looked at me, her eyes sparkled with passion, I was certain I was a strong and powerful man. If a woman cried for me, I believed without a doubt that I was loved. When she turned away from me, frowned, or disapproved of me or my actions, I simply found my way to another woman's smile. I wasn't surprised or ashamed when I realized this truth about myself. I was after all a boy child raised exclusively by a woman.

When my mother smiled at me I knew that I was loved. When her eyes sparkled with approval at my schoolwork or a song I had sung I felt like the most perfect little boy in the world. When Mom frowned and became angry I feared that both our relationship and her love for me were at risk. The problem was that as I attempted to journey toward manhood I continued to use the boyhood yardstick of my worth as the primary measure of my worthiness as a man.

"Man, if I put you on an island for one year with no women on it, you'd die."

"What are you talking about?" I protested.

"I'm saying you'd probably die if you had to live without women."

Words began mobilizing themselves in my head preparing a defense against my friend's brutal assault upon my character. None of the words, however, got farther than my throat. Instead, out of my mouth came wave after wave of grateful laughter. He was right. While I might not actually die a physical death in an environment with no women, I would, to say the least, have great difficulty maintaining a healthy dose of self-esteem. A few years ago if someone had put me on a woman-less island, even seeing my own reflection in a pool of crystal blue water might not have been enough for me to say convincingly: "I am somebody."

It's good to have friends who care about you enough to

kick you in the seat of the pants hard enough to land you smack dab on the problem. The landing may hurt a little. But once you've landed squarely on the problem you might begin to catch a glimpse of the solution.

These days I rarely use the eyes of others as the primary measure of my self-worth. Today I figure I could last maybe a whole five years on that island. That may not be perfection but it sure is a pocketful of progress. Today it is "progress" that I use to measure myself: if I'm farther up the road than I was yesterday, I'm okay with that. I still use a mirror sometimes. It's the one in my bathroom. Each morning, if I can stand and look myself directly in the eye, then it's a good day.

fatherhood

There is a man in my house
He's so big and strong
He goes to work each day and stays all day long
Comes home at night, looking tired and beat
I think I'll color him Father
I think I'll color him love.

—O.C. SMITH

When my son was born I believed his birth to be a trap set by an evil self-serving woman, a woman whose real motive was to prevent me from continuing on my fun-filled and exciting path toward "manhood." The truth is, I was not so much a victim as I was a volunteer. Because I had come to depend so heavily on women to boost my self-esteem I had, through my own need, deliberately placed myself in a position to become a travel partner in another human being's journey toward womanhood.

If you look at women the way society often does—as second class and not quite the equal of men—then you may not realize that girls must make a journey too. The old saying "Behind every man, there's a good woman" leads us to believe that a woman's purpose in life is to follow a man as he makes his journey. To offer him comfort; something nice to look at; someone to make the ol' campfire and rustle up the grub. We may even look at our own mothers and conclude that their primary role was to give us a good start and then stay behind holding down the homestead waiting for our triumphant return. While I was in the Marine Corps, Georgia decided to do a bit of remodeling on our house. She went to the library, checked out a remodeling book, drove to Sears and bought some tools, and then transformed my room into a den. She also built a deck. Here I was, a military veteran from the dangerous beaches and blue water of Puerto Rico, home from the peacetime wars. Instead of ticker tape, a parade, and a tearful mother in an apron grateful for my return, I came home to find a woman who had continued to take great strides on her own journey. And who, soon after I arrived, retired to chill out on her deck. A few years later Mom enrolled at a local university to finish her undergraduate work. I'm ashamed to say it, but I didn't understand why she needed to go back to school. I didn't realize that after spending so many years preparing me to make *my* mark she was preparing to make her mark as well. I was the journeyman, the traveler, the doer. She was supposed to be the proud mother, stationary, waiting— fulfilled and content in her own life thanks to the success and achievement in mine.

Today I understand a little better that a woman too must make her own journey. A portion of her travels may include being of service to me as I move along. Just as my journey may include being of service to her and others. However, a woman's journey is not about my destinations but about the destinations she chooses for herself. And the map of my experience has shown me that a woman may choose as her destination healing the sick, running a corporation or a nation, supporting a husband, or gaining a spot in the NBA. The map of my experience has also shown me that in addition to those destinations and others many women will also choose motherhood as a milestone on their journey.

So there I went, on my way, making my journey. I met a woman; she was traveling too. We decided to travel a few miles together. We both enjoyed the other's company but rarely did we talk about our individual destinations. Because we were traveling together I somehow assumed (perhaps we both did) that we were headed for the same destination. One day as we walked along laughing and enjoying the journey, the woman stopped, turned to me, and smiled. "Well, here we are," she announced.

"Here we are, where?" I asked pleasantly.

"At our destination, silly," she replied, nudging my arm.

"Oh. Okay. So where are we?" I asked again. As the woman set her backpack down and began unpacking her things I just happened to look up. There, overhead, was a big flashing neon sign that read: WELCOME TO THE LAND OF MOTHERHOOD! GOOD LUCK!

"Hey! Hey! What's this?" I asked. "I mean, how did we get here?" I'm shocked and angry. She, on the other hand, was looking at me as if I were crazy.

"What are you talking about?" she asked, more than a little hurt. "We've been traveling together for a while. I thought you were making my journey with me."

"Making my journey with you? What are you saying? I thought you were traveling with me!" I couldn't believe this was happening. I paced back and forth trying to figure out how I was going to get out of there. I was thinking: "Hey, I don't belong here. I wasn't headed here in the first place.

"I can't believe that you've brought me here," I told my friend accusingly. "I can't believe you tricked me into coming to this . . . this place! This land of . . ."

Just then I looked up again, back toward that flashing sign. I realized I'd missed something. That neon sign, you see, alternated. First it flashed one greeting and then another. This time as I looked up the sign flashed, WELCOME TO THE LAND OF FATHERHOOD! GOOD LUCK!

When my son was conceived I had absolutely no intention of even visiting the land of fatherhood. I did, however, spend some time journeying with the woman who would soon be his mother. Denise had been on her journey for many years when we met. She'd made it to many of her destinations too: college, a good career, and some really solid friendships. I on the other hand was still trudging toward several of my life goals (in between trips to the Loaded). One day while we were journeying together Denise told me quite openly that she was ready to have a child. I stopped what I was doing, looked at Denise, and thought about what she had said for a moment. Then I promptly concluded that she wasn't at all serious. So I smiled, nodded, and went on about my business.

Denise and I had met at a nightclub. She was cute, friendly, and lots of fun. After a couple of dates I discovered that she was also smart and kind. We never made any sort of formal decision to journey together. We didn't have to. The fact that we were spending so much time together pretty much meant that we had become temporary travel partners. To Denise, however, the nature of our companionship was considerably more permanent. I don't recall ever asking Denise what her destinations were, what she wanted out of life, or even where she was headed the night we met. Still, in time, Denise was honest with me about her destination. "I'm ready to have a child," she had said. It's not that I didn't hear her, it's just that I wasn't listening. I didn't realize she was holding out a map of her journey and where she intended to go. I thought I was the only one with such a map.

Because I didn't think of women as on their own journeys, it barely occurred to me that Denise was a traveler. So, when she said, "I'm ready to have a child," what I heard was: "Greg-Alan, are you ready to have a child? The answer to the question I had heard was, of course, no. In truth, however, Denise wasn't asking me about my journey. Denise was telling me where she was headed on her own journey. Gentlemen, girls and women are people too! They have goals and dreams and agendas all their own. When a woman speaks, listen. Most of the time, when a man speaks to you he is trying to tell you about himself and his journey. A woman is no different. A few years ago I met a professional salesman who shared with me what he considered to be one of the central secrets of success at selling. Here's what he said:

> "When I go into a client's office to make a sale I'm well acquainted with the products I have to offer. I know my products' many features, their advantages over the competition's products. But instead of launching right in and trying to convince the client that I've got the best products on the market, I spend a substantial amount of time asking questions and listening to the answers. If I'm selling copying machines, for example, I ask the client questions like: How many copies do you make per week? What percentage of those are color copies? What kind of copying does your office normally do? Single sheets or multiple page documents? The answers to these questions give me a pretty good idea of which one of my copiers would

work best for that client. I've learned over the years that if you listen to people long enough eventually they will tell you exactly what they want you to sell them."

The map of this salesman's journey has served me again and again in lots of situations. Because of that map I know today that if I listen to a person long enough he will tell me what he needs. Just like the salesman's client, if I listen well enough, a woman will tell me where she's headed on her journey. Even if she doesn't really mean to. Listening means shutting up and laying my plans aside and letting the other person do the talking. Listening means asking questions and then waiting patiently for the answers. Listening means that becoming a woman's travel partner the moment you meet her is not a good idea. Listening, asking questions, truly hearing another person takes time.

Whether or not a woman has actually marked motherhood as a destination on her journey, she can become a mother almost anytime during her travels. And that means that boys and men can become fathers anytime too. It happens. Women are by nature capable of getting pregnant anytime without prior notice to anyone. And when a woman arrives at the land of motherhood, either intentionally or unintentionally, she never arrives alone. The father of the child always arrives with her. He may leave the woman, but he can never leave that land once his child enters the world. A man may even leave his child. But he will remain a father nonetheless. A man may be a responsible father or he may be an irresponsible father but he will always be a father. The question is: if a man is a father and is not being a father, is he really a man?

This question has nothing to do with the mother of the child or her journey. This question is solely about you and your child. Once you are a father, how you arrived at fatherhood (intentionally or unintentionally) is no longer an issue as it relates to your child. Having another human being growing inside you must be a pretty deep experience. And, I suspect, that there is no act of creation greater than giving birth. A man or a woman may build a building, discover a cure for AIDS, write a book or a song. But what could be greater than carrying and releasing life itself? Giving birth to another being is something a man will never experience. It is important, however, to remember that women do not create the life they are carrying inside of themselves alone. It takes both a man and a woman to create life.

Women and men are equals. In some ways we are the same, but in many ways we are quite different. In the matter of babies, unmarried men and unmarried women are often miles apart. But whether or not a woman has made motherhood a destination on her journey the most important thing for us to remember is: a man must maintain his power of choice over when and with whom he will create a child. Once your sperm is released it is too late to change your mind.

Gentleman, when you become a father, don't try to hide from the truth of your fatherhood. There is no place to hide. None of us can hide from the G.O.D. that lives in all of us. There is an expression that says: there's a bit of bad in the best of us and a bit of good in the worst of us. G.O.D. is that "best" that lives even in the worst of men. G.O.D. is the best in us that will not allow our heads to forget that we are fathers. There will be many days when thoughts of your child will cross your mind. You'll wonder what he looks like. If she's doing okay. You'll wonder what the child would be like if it had you around as a father. You may be able to block these thoughts for a while. Perhaps even for many years. But as you grow older, quiet thoughts of your child and much louder thoughts from your own conscience will creep up on you many a day, making you sad and ashamed.

For a long time a fire wall of fear stood between me and my son. We lived in different cities so it was hard for us to see each other regularly. But instead of visiting now and then and maybe taking in the park, or the zoo, or a game of catch, I didn't visit at all. I was afraid that he would dislike me for not visiting more often. Early in my acting career I wasn't making much money. I moved around a lot, and I knew that being a father was a big responsibility. I was afraid I couldn't cut it, so I didn't try. I was ashamed because I wasn't earning the kind of money I thought I needed to support a child. Rather than sending the small regular amounts I could afford, I sent nothing at all. For a long time I didn't call or write my son. I shut myself off from our relationship and my responsibility as a man and as a father. My fear of not being the perfect father with lots of money to support my son caused me not to suit up and show up for that leg of my journey called fatherhood.

Friends, it was just about this time that I discovered that shame follows fear. With my son, what began as the fear of the responsibilities that came with fatherhood, soon became shame for my shortcomings as a father. Clearly the best thing to do would have been to send whatever amount of money I could afford each week. But fear and shame drove me further and further away from both my son and a solution.

Each new day brought a fresh opportunity to be a better father than I had been the day before. But instead of starting new each day, I was too scared, and then ashamed, and I'd always fail to suit up and show up for life. I was what folks call nowadays "a deadbeat dad." My failure as a father became my most closely guarded secret. I was afraid of what people would think of me if they found out. And while I was worrying about something that silly, time was passing—important time that I could have been spending with my son. I was like that guy standing with one foot in California and the other foot in New York. I had one foot all the way in yesterday's shame, another foot all the way in tomorrow's fear, and the present—the time I should have been spending with my son—was running right through my legs.

As my fire wall of fear got hotter and hotter I cooled my conscience with a drink, or smothered my shame with a joint. With the help of a little weed and a little wine I made up a world in which I was not a failed father, but a victim of a selfish woman's attempt to trap me into marriage and a boring life. Even though I still couldn't look myself straight in the eye, when I was loaded it was easier for me to hide from my fear and think my son really didn't need me. After all, I had grown up without a father in my house and look at me. I worked, sometimes I excelled. I took care of myself. I was okay and my son would be too. When I stepped into an environment shaped by drugs and/or alcohol, my thinking easily slipped past my fear and shame, and past the few painful memories of what it was like growing up without a father. Or how hard it was sometimes for Mom to take care of me all by herself. Or how important it was for me that Mr. Blue was around most of my life. A guy who took me fishing and hunting, frowned at me when I said something silly, shook me when I did something stupid, and reminded me to respect my mom and to respect myself. Mr. Blue was not *always* there but the memory of missing him in our house so many days and nights will never leave me. Because of that memory I knew that as my son grew he would miss me too. But growing up without a regular live-in Dad and turning out "okay" as an adult helped me ignore the *very real* experience of my own boyhood and strengthened my belief that my son would grow up fine without me.

Through the years that I failed to be a good father I conjured up images of myself that were hip, slick, and very much "the man." But the truth is I wasn't very much "the man" at all and I certainly wasn't all that okay, especially if I failed to understand that a son needs a father to become a man; and that a father must be a father to be a man. Growing up, I was surrounded by images that celebrated the beauty of birth: the

Blessed Virgin cradling her child in a manger; the glowing young mother smiling down upon her newborn in a hospital bed or prairie cabin; the courageous mother enduring indescribable pain to bring her child into the world; baby pictures of me with my mom. In most of these scenes the father of the baby looks on in the background, humble and helpless. Old movies show the young father outside the delivery room, pacing back and forth, wringing his hands while the mother and the doctor go about their difficult and valuable business. In some birth scenarios, including my own, men were absent altogether. Of course, from a fairly young age I knew that a man was needed to create a new life, but only during the recent years of my journey have I begun to understand the tremendous importance of that role. You see, I grew up believing that the miracle of life lay not in the planting, but only in the harvest. I entered manhood thinking that there was no miracle in my role in creating new life. I am only now beginning to understand that my sperm, the seed needed to fertilize the female egg, is as precious as the egg itself. My body neither carries nor bears a child. Still, my body and my role in creating life, are irreplaceable; they are as beautiful and as sacred as a woman's.

All too often, when I was growing up, a man's role in the creation of life was depicted as dirty. A man who had impregnated an unmarried woman was said to have gotten her "in trouble." Little boys who were curious about their sexual roles were called "nasty" by girls and adults alike. And despite the ridicule received from family and friends, once an unmarried pregnant girl gave birth she seemed to automatically ascend in her own mind and in the minds of many others to a divine but difficult state of grace called motherhood.

Motherhood is indeed a difficult and divine calling, a calling that demands sacrifice, patience, and compassion. But what about fatherhood? In our society, becoming a father may not automatically get you a kind of lightweight sainthood. But being a good father demands the same kind of commitment, compassion, and perseverance as motherhood. Sadly, many of the messages we get while we're growing up tell us that as males (made of "snakes and snails and puppy dogs' tails") we are not beautiful makers of babies and an important, primary part of our child's upbringing. Only recently have I come to appreciate the truth that the "planting of our seed is precious and important."

Women are taught and encouraged to be very selective and cautious about whom they make love with. Boys on the other hand are rarely so advised. "Get as much as you can while you can," were the words whispered to me when I was a very young man. Even Mr. Blue grinned broadly when I told him of my first sexual encounter. No one, including myself, ever asked where, why, or with whom I had left the seed capable of creating new life. In leaving my seed where I had no desire or intention to create a child I was totally abandoning my power of choice in the matter of when and with whom I would create a child.

Certainly I was warned about getting girls pregnant. But no one, however, ever warned me about getting me pregnant! That's because males don't carry babies in their bodies. Remember, however, the miracle, beauty, and, most of all, the *responsibility* of birth lies not only in the harvest (the birth of the child) but also in the planting (the conception of that child). There is life inside us too, gentlemen! This seed, this potential for life, is as serious and valuable as a woman's ability to carry and release a child into the world. We must respect the power we have to give life. The best way to respect that power is to abstain from sex until we become adults. Until we are ready to assume the responsibilities of being a father. Once we choose a travel partner, using a condom is essential at all times. Birth control is your responsibility, not the woman's with whom you are traveling. It is your responsibility to choose your journey's direction and destinations.

education

*Service is the rent you pay for room
on this earth.*

—SHIRLEY CHISHOLM

When I was growing up I used to hear people say, "Knowledge is power." I was taught that a high school diploma and a college degree (or two) would make me invincible. Most of the folks in my neighborhood believed that if a guy was born poor and underprivileged, a solid education was the key to getting out of the "hood." As a high school junior, I took extra courses at night so that I could graduate early, then get to college and get on with the business of getting myself some knowledge and some "power." I wanted to get away from Mom and into the power-filled world of men as quickly as possible—a world I defined primarily in terms of money and prestige. I graduated from high school at the end of my junior year and earned a partial scholarship to a small college in Iowa. That summer I worked weighing trucks for the state highway commission, then, in August, I began my journey into higher education.

When I began I liked most of my freshman courses. A couple of classes you could even call exciting. I discovered that in college you were encouraged to form opinions and share your ideas about the subject you were studying. Most of my professors paid their students a level of respect I had rarely enjoyed during high school. Still, while the respect of my teachers and the challenge of my coursework felt good, the respect of my peers and feeling "hip, slick, and cool" meant a whole lot more. So, as I told you earlier, soon after I started college, I also started slipping over to the Loaded. You'll recall that over in the Loaded it was easy to imagine myself as a truly powerful guy. All it took to get that feeling was five or ten dollars, the cost of a bag of weed or a few bottles of wine. On the real side, over in the Straight, attending classes, studying, doing homework, gaining the power that I believed came with knowledge, required a lot more effort. So, within three or four months after starting college I was spending more time imagining and dreaming about the man I thought I was and the man I thought I wanted to become than actually making the journey toward becoming a man.

While I was journeying over to the Loaded, most of the other kids were journeying to class, every day getting closer to becoming the men and women they wanted to be. As I look back, however, I don't believe it was the weed and the wine and the hanging out at the dance clubs that actually prevented me from making it to class or getting my homework done. The weed, the wine, and the all-night parties were only symptoms of my problem. The real problem was my reason for attending college in the first place.

Most people go to college so that they can get a good job when they graduate. A solid career can make a man's journey much more pleasant. With a good job, you can pay your rent and buy groceries, a nice car, and hip clothes. In time you may even be able to buy a house and travel around the world. We journey to college, to trade school, and to apprenticeship programs so we can develop some skills. Then we take those skills and apply them to our work. Our skills (our work) are what we give to the world in exchange for currency (cash), which we use to purchase the things we need on our journey. In this world, we are not allowed to print our own money. Instead we have to trade things for it, our "services," our work and our skills. Sometimes I receive cash for my services, and sometimes I receive the services of others. Without skills to exchange, I will have little of what I need for my own journey. The primary purpose of higher education, then, is to provide us with skills with which we can serve others. If this is true then what I failed to understand so many years ago was that college is not so much about gaining power and prestige but is more about figuring out how to be of maximum service to others. For me, it was about developing skills I could use to be of service.

Most of us think of service as time and energy we offer others without the expectation of receiving money in return. The truth, however, is that all work whether performed in exchange for a fee or offered free of charge constitutes service.

Lots of folks make their dollars providing services that enhance our lives. Others serve their communities in ways that destroy. The doctor serves the sick. The volunteer Scout leader serves the needs of boys and young men. But the thief serves too: he serves those who would buy the stolen possessions of others at a discount. The dope dealer is of service to the dope fiend. There is nothing wrong with receiving money in exchange for the good and productive work you offer others. However, when you offer a service that is negative or destructive, in time you will suffer the ill effects of the ugliness you've given. And if you look around you will see that dope dealers don't deal long. Eventually the destruction they sell comes back to their own lives in the form of death, incarceration, and addiction. People, however, who act in ways that benefit others can serve honorably and productively until the day they die. For example, a teacher, an anthropologist, or a dentist, these folks provide a service to others that is intended not only to better their own lives but others as well.

As a child in church I was taught that the poor were blessed, the rich cursed and evil. These days you let a wealthy man come along who appears to be a pretty decent person and plenty of people may hold him suspect simply because he is rich. "Naw, this guy can't be on the real. He's got too much paper. He's got to be up to something." Nice guys didn't get rich, I thought; most successful and wealthy people had to have a little slick in 'em, rich folks were selfish and exploited others.

It is hard for me to accept the image of the well-to-do "good guy." But the image of the rich crook is fairly easy for me to swallow. But gentlemen, principle and profit are compatible! You can be a good and honorable man, of service to others and, if you choose, *make money at it!* The currency we receive in exchange for our service is a measure of the value of our service, and it is okay to take pride in receiving this money for work well done. It doesn't make our service less valuable.

Sure we all expect to get paid for our labor, but in order to get paid we must first have something to give, to serve. Sort of like a restaurant. You've got to have more than tables, chairs, and nice atmosphere to run a successful eatery. There's got to be something on the menu, something good and tasty that your customers will truly savor. As I entered college, my mind should have been set on developing my "menu" of skills—a menu that others would find useful in their own lives. Does a surgeon study medicine for eight to twelve years so he can eventually operate on himself? Does a carpenter learn his trade so that he may one day build houses that only he will live in? No way. Both the doctor and the carpenter develop their skills so that they can serve others with those skills.

All of us have dreams, destinations we want to reach on our journey. Usually our destinations are extremely far away, and it becomes difficult for us to see them even in our imaginations. Sometimes when we can no longer summon in our hearts and minds the picture of their fulfillment, the excitement or the joy that we believe will come by reaching our destination, we slow down and become discouraged and perhaps even abandon our dreams completely. Or, as in the case of my travels to the Loaded, we may look for dangerous, self-destructive ways to make the image of our destinations (and our ideal future selves) more vivid and real. These actions actually slow us down even more and, in fact, send us in directions far away from our intended destination.

Even before you get to college, trade school, or an apprenticeship, right now in high school, middle school, and junior high, when schoolwork starts getting you down, when it gets harder and harder to participate or to pay attention in class, remember that your journey through school is meant primarily to take you to a place in your life where you can be of much-needed service to the world.

As you change your focus to serving others, go find those that you could serve. If you intend to become a teacher, spend time among those who cannot read or among those who have difficulty learning. Spend time with these people and with the teachers who serve them: there you will certainly see clearly the great need for your service. You may also get a deeper sense of what is required to be of service as a teacher and learn of rewards, other than money, your services may reap. Or if, for example, you want to become a builder but the road to that destination is looking harder and harder and you begin to doubt that you can cut it, head downtown. Head downtown and walk among those hundreds and thousands of folks who live in cardboard boxes. Visit a freeway underpass and say hello to the folks who live there. Even though you may doubt your own ability to master the skills necessary to be of service, once you see so many who desperately need a roof over their head, once you get a sense of just how many people need safe, warm places to live, you may be inspired to study a little harder. The sight of the homeless may motivate you to stick to your goal for another day. The opportunity to serve those homeless folks may move you closer toward your intended goal.

While some form of higher education—trade school, college, or apprenticeship—is a part of most young men's future these days, the skills we acquire in higher education grow out of the skills we are developing right now in middle school, junior high, and high school. Competency in English and math, an appreciation of history, an understanding of the fundamentals of science, these things are key to developing our ability to be of service to others. Without these basic skills, our ability to be of maximum service will be seriously diminished.

In fact the basic skills you've already learned and are learning as students today can even help you be of service right now. If you possess a thorough understanding of addition, subtraction, multiplication, and division, there are many people younger than yourself, and even older than you, whom you can serve with that skill. If you're a good reader, I guarantee you there are literacy programs in your community that could use your knowledge right now in helping others to learn to read. If you possess athletic skills and a strong body, there are elders who could use a strong arm to hold just so they can take a walk in a garden or get their groceries home from the store. Many of these folks you can serve may not have money to offer in exchange for your services. But if you make service the purpose of your learning, you may find the currency you receive in exchange for your skills is as valuable as cash money.

We all have to go to school, study, and learn. If we expand the focus for *why* we're doing this from ourselves to include serving others we will see that in exchange for our service we get much in return personally as well as financially. The first requirement of the exchange, however, is that we have a menu of skills which we can offer to others. Education, learning from the cradle to the grave, is an essential component of our journey simply because we cannot offer to others what we do not have ourselves.

baggage

To accept one's past—one's history—
is not the same thing as drowning in it;
it is learning how to use it.

—JAMES BALDWIN

You know, it seems that whenever I go on a long trip out of town I come back with more stuff than I went out with. The longer I travel the more stuff I collect. Sometimes I have to pick up an extra bag just to carry all that stuff home. My journey's been that way too. With each step of my journey I collect more information and experiences, many that are good and others that are not so good. The information and experiences find their way onto my maps and the maps go into the bags I carry with me. Over the course of my journey I've collected all kinds of things: joy, pain, anger, rage, understanding, a pinch of patience, and a little humility. Like all travelers I started out on my journey with a set of bags. The bags I began my journey with were filled with some of my mother's experiences. Things she shared with me about her journey, her parents' journey, and so on. Very early I received bits and pieces of maps from other people such as teachers, playmates, ministers and aunts and from television, movies, and other places. I even got maps from dead people; the stories of their lives passed down to me from family and books. The list is endless.

A few of the maps I received from others were filled with mountains of hardship, horror, unfairness, hatred, and unreachable destinations. For years I collected maps like this in more and more bags and carried them with me. Maps of black folks' experiences as slaves and second-class citizens. Maps of Africans dying in seagoing coffins. I carried maps of scenes from the civil rights movement I had watched on television as I grew up. These maps were filled with beatings, fire bombings, bigotry, and great victories. I carried these maps stuffed right in alongside the maps of my own difficult experiences with bigotry and racism. On those days when I would run into an obstacle built by racism I'd stop and dig into my bags in the hope of finding a map that might show me how to climb over or around the hatred. Many times I'd pull out maps that were familiar to me. Maps I had studied before. Maps others had used that gave a clear picture of the rugged terrain in the land of racism. Let's say one was a map of my grandfather's experience as given to me by my mom. The other was a map of a black woman's experience I had gotten from a book. After looking over my grandad's map for a few minutes I'd easily conclude that there was simply no way to get past the obstacle. But then, I'd turn to the second map, the one found in the book—a different kind of map of an African-American woman's experience in the land of racism. As I'd study that map I'd discover that she had found a way past the obstacle! The path she had been forced to take was straight up the mountain. The route was brutal and hazardous. Still she had gotten up and over the obstacle and continued her journey. Now I'd be excited and hopeful, so I'd read on. Then, only a few pages farther, I'd be shocked to find that many more huge obstacles had been constructed in the path of this courageous and resourceful African-American's journey. Angry then, I'd feel quite hopeless. With those maps clenched tightly in my hand I'd raise my rage toward the mountain in my way and shake my fist. I'd shout, "See what you did! Do you see what you did to my grandfather and to this courageous African-American woman! Do you see what you're doing to me! Do you see? Do you see?"

I've been lucky on my journey. In those moments when I've stood shaking my fist at the mountain other journeymen and women have come along and helped me get a grip.

"Do you see that?" I ask them. "Look what they've placed in my path. I'll never get to my destination with that thing in the way. It's huge. How am I going to get past it?"

"What maps are you using?" the journeyman asks calmly.

"These," I reply, unwrinkling the maps and opening them on the ground.

"These maps look awfully old," says the journeyman, examining them closely.

"Yes, but they're good and honest maps. One belongs to my grandfather. He was a good man. And the other belongs to a woman I read about in a book. Every time she figured out how to get past one obstacle, another was thrown in her path."

"Yes. Yes I can see that," mumbles the journeyman, still poring over the old maps. "Listen, I tell you what, let's take a look in your bags."

"What for?" I ask defensively.

"Just to see what other maps you might have in there. Is that okay?"

I acquiesce and together we start digging through all of those bags of mine, looking for some more maps. As we dig I noticed that the journeyman who has stopped to help is carrying only one, maybe two bags at best. His bags are full but his maps aren't bulging out all over the place like mine. Yet it's clear that this journeyman has been on the road for some time. "Where are all his bags?" I wonder.

"Here's one, two, three, four . . . Yes!" the journeyman announces, pulling a number of fresh-looking maps from my bags. "Here's what we're looking for. I think these will do just fine." The journeyman kneels and spreads the maps out over the ground. A few of the points on the maps look vaguely familiar but I can't recall the last time I'd even looked at any of the maps.

"According to these maps," says the journeyman, "there are several ways to get past this mountain."

"Where? Show me," I challenge with a smirk.

"Here are a couple of clearly marked paths up and over the mountain," he says, tracing the paths with a finger. "In fact there are symbols here that indicate several different types of vehicles you can actually ride over the mountain. On this map here, you'll find a couple of trails that lead around the mountain. And, if I'm not mistaken, this other map shows what looks like a tunnel that will take you comfortably beneath the mountain itself to the other side."

I lean over to take a good long look at the maps. I study them closely for a minute and sure enough the journeyman is right. These maps clearly show lots of ways to get beyond the mountain of racism. "This is amazing. How did you know about these other maps?" I ask. "I didn't even realize they were in my bags."

"That's probably because you're so familiar with the maps of your grandfather and the woman from the book. When you come upon the mountain of racism you automatically pull out those old maps. The ones you're used to seeing. These maps here are a lot more recent. There's rugged terrain here too and still a lot of uphill going, but not nearly so much as was on your grandfather's map or on the map of that courageous African-American woman.''

There have been many days on my journey when I pulled out those old maps and swore that they were a good and true representation of the terrain I was standing on. Thank goodness those other journey folks helped me go back through my bags to see if there were any other maps in there that might give me a more current picture of racist terrain. Here in America bigotry and racism can still present an uphill climb for black folk. Just as sexism, homophobia, age discrimination, anti-Semitism, and other forms of intolerance create huge obstacles for all kinds of folks. Obstacles quite often as big and broad as any obstacle faced by folks of color. More recent maps from the journeys of people of color clearly show us that there are many more ways to get beyond this mountain than there were for our grandmothers and grandfathers. Just look at all the destinations on those recent maps. Destinations that weren't even considered by earlier journeymen. These new destinations include running the entire armed forces, sitting on the Supreme Court, owning and managing major corporations, playing professional sports, selling billions of records and keeping most of the profits, journeying into space, and almost any other destination you can think of. Destinations in business, sports, science, entertainment, law, politics, literature, and on and on. And to think there were days not long ago when men and women of color weren't able to choose their own destinations, let alone prepare themselves and actually head out for those destinations. Today, when I confront obstacles of intolerance I may still retrieve my grandfather's maps, but I also pull out these newer maps as well. I take all those maps and place them alongside the map of my own experience as I figure out how to make my way beyond the mountain.

When I honestly compare the map of my experience with my grandfather's map it becomes quite clear that there is a difference in the terrain. Take, for example, the issue of higher education. Let's say I'm standing in the land of college. As I stand there I ask myself, "How will I get in? Where can I go to school? I'm poor. How will I pay my tuition?" All right. Now I pull out my grandfather's map, the one I'm familiar with. The one people have talked about so much. I lift that map from the top of one of my bags and give it the once-over. Oh boy— according to Grandfather's map, the land of college looks like a pretty desolate place. I see a lot of colleges and universities on the map but most of them are marked "whites only." I see a few colleges though that will admit a journeyman of color, but only a few. And even the colleges that will admit my grandfather and me cost money. Lots of money. After looking at this map I conclude that, like my grandfather, there is absolutely no way for me to get beyond this mountain. But wait a minute. How old is this map? The terrain I see there may have been true for my grandfather but is this map a true depiction of the terrain on my journey today? Not quite. To get a clear picture of the land of college for my journey today I need to find maps of more recent experience. As I study more recent maps I will see that nearly all of those once "whites only" schools *will* accept journeymen of color. When I look even closer I find that there are many paths marked with dollar signs that lead to places where I can borrow or earn the money to pay for my college education. As far as giving an accurate picture of how I should travel today, my grandfather's map may mislead me. If I use only that old map to guide me I may mistakenly conclude that a black man has no chance in America.

But not all maps of recent experience support the notion that a black man can make a good and useful journey in America. All of us can find contemporary journeymen who will tell us sincerely that the terrain of racism on their journey is insurmountable. It may be that some of the maps you have gathered so far strongly suggest that this is true: that the mountains of poverty and racism are unconquerable, that a black man can't get a break in America, and that a poor man is out of luck and beaten before he begins. What about those maps of experience? How should we consider them? Here, gentlemen, is where the art of cross-referencing is essential. Before you accept the accuracy of any map that tells you that your destination is unreachable, cross-reference. Do some research. If you have even read or heard somewhere about a man or woman of color making it over or around that mountain, search them out. Write them a letter. Pay them a visit. Stand in a line and wait for your chance to ask them about the map of their experience. If you dream of being a doctor and someone tells you that you can't get to that destination, before you accept that information as gospel ask around. See if there are any doctors of color anywhere on the planet. If you can find one, just one, go see her. Write her a letter. Ask her to share with you how she got to her destination. Ask her to point out the mountains of intolerance she came upon. Ask her how she got beyond them. Then take some time to reflect and compare her maps with the maps of others. Compare the route of her journey with the routes of others who have told you that because they were poor, black, brown, or white they could not reach their intended destinations. If you examine each of those maps closely, you may find that it was not simply the obstacles of intolerance that blocked the way of so many folks, but obstacles built by the journeymen themselves that played key roles in preventing them from reaching their destinations. Likewise, if you're able to find another person not so different from yourself, who has reached his destination you will probably discover that they have played a key role in their journey by keeping self-made obstacles to a minimum and by calling for help when they found an obstacle too tough to handle. All of us play a key role in reaching our own destinations.

Brothers, beware of folks who hand you maps marked primarily with failure. Although failure can help us learn how to make more useful journeys, a map filled with failure alone will not guide us well. Beware of maps that are filled with anger and bitterness. These feelings blur the information on any map. Anger and bitterness are born inside of tears and hurt. Hurt is the father of anger and the mother of bitterness. The anger and bitterness we feel are literally frozen hardened tears sitting on our hearts and in our eyes. Try looking through an ice cube sometime. Everything on the other side will be out of focus. A blur. Studying any map through a lens of anger and bitterness will leave us blind to the reality of our destinations and the terrain ahead of us. Cross-reference. Be certain your destination is truly unreachable before giving up on that destination.

Remember too that even though the old maps may not contain a lot of accurate information they are still useful and you should never throw them away. If nothing else, the difficult terrain they show can serve to remind you of the kinds of obstacles human beings willingly build in the paths of others. They can also remind you of the kinds of obstacles people place in their own paths. And since you too are a human being, these same maps can teach you what you are capable of. The information we get from these maps is very important; however, I don't believe that we have to carry them with us all the time. You may recall that when the journeyman stopped to help me look inside my bags for more recent and more accurate maps, I noticed that he was carrying only one or two bags. One of the important lessons I've learned from other successful travelers is that I don't have to stuff my bags with all the maps I've gathered. And I certainly don't need to carry those maps every step of my journey.

Most of my maps need to be kept on a shelf somewhere, readily accessible at all times for study and reflection. This is particularly true with the maps of horror and hardship. You see I need those maps—the experiences of my grandfather and that courageous woman—however, I can't be carrying that stuff with me all the time. The more of those maps I carry the heavier my bags become. The heavier my bags, the harder it is to travel. Have you ever seen a guy in an airport with a whole bunch of bags? The man is all hunched over, sweatin'. His clothes are wrinkled and he has to stop every few feet just to rest. It's the same way with some of those folks who push those shopping carts. The cart will be piled high and wide with stuff. It's so heavy they can hardly get it across the street and up over the curb. They have trouble guiding the cart and making it go in the direction they want it to go. They've got too much stuff, too many of those plastic garbage bags. Too many bags—too many maps in our bags—weigh us down and make it difficult for us to travel well. You see, there's something about those maps, something that affects us even when we're not looking at them. It's like the weight of the maps, the experiences and information on them, gets inside us and makes us want to cry. Of course we're men and we don't cry so our tears turn to ice and lock the anger and bitterness inside. It weighs on our hearts and makes us cold. Weighs us down, slows us down, and often keeps us down. And the longer we're down the more hopeless we may feel. In fact I sometimes think that's what might be wrong with the people who live out of those carts. Long before they started putting all that stuff in the carts maybe they were putting every one of the maps they found in their bags. Until finally, over time, the weight of those maps, of hard experience and hurt—their own and others'—simply dragged them down until they were too tired to get up. I used to watch those folks with the carts, just like I watched the Commodity Kid in the car across the alley. I genuinely feared that one day I'd end up pushing one of those carts. I used to look out the window of that radio station in Los Angeles and see a guy across the street, oily, dirty, talking to himself. I couldn't make out his face clearly because of the distance. But what I could see of his face seemed to resemble my own, with a beard, without a bath or a destination. Since then I've learned to leave a lot of my heavy baggage on a shelf, in a drawer, somewhere I can get to it when I need it, but someplace where it won't weigh me down.

These days the bags I travel with are filled primarily with the maps of my own experience and the more recent maps of the experiences of others. The journey is always changing, though, so I keep exchanging older maps for newer ones. Updating as I go, yet rarely discarding any map in its entirety. I travel light. One day's journey at a time. One foot in front of the other. You see, this book is nearly done now, in a moment I will reach my destination. I've traveled here to the end. One letter, one word, one sentence at a time. There are more destinations to be reached. But for the moment I think I'll set my bags down and rest.